THE

ELEMENTS

of STYLE

GRAMMAR WORKBOOK

THE ELEMENTS of STYLE

GRAMMAR WORKBOOK

RICHARD DE A'MORELLI,
EDITOR

SPECTRUM INK PUBLISHING

The Elements of Style: Grammar Workbook

Spectrum Ink Publishing
Email: Editor@Spectrum.org
Phone: 1-805-888-2900
Website: https://books.spectrum.org/

ISBN Numbers:

978-1-64399-008-8	Paperback (Amazon)
978-1-64399-009-5	Kindle Edition (MOBI)
978-1-64399-007-1	Nook/iStore/Google (EPUB)
978-1-64399-005-7	Ingram Paperback
978-1-64399-006-4	Ingram Hardcover

Spectrum Ink Publishing
Houston, Texas ~ San Luis Obispo, California

Dedication

This book is dedicated to my long-lost and finally-found sister, Joan Carole Finkes, and her loving husband, David, who opened their hearts and their home to me, and shared their lives with me during much of 2018. Joan and I spent most of our adult lives searching for one another, I believing that she had died of multiple sclerosis when I was eight, according to a nutty fiction told by my mother, and she assuming that I had been killed in Viet Nam. Discovering that I had a sister, alive and well in Texas, was a wonderful surprise, and it came at a time in my life when I needed it most, just a few months before my only child was killed in a botched robbery attempt. Knowing that I was not alone in this world and had a sister and family who cared helped me get through that trauma.

I am glad we finally connected (through the Ancestry.com website) and that we had a chance to spend quality time getting to know one another. It is not possible to make up for a lifetime of missed experiences and memories that we might have shared growing up together, but we can both imagine how it might have been and be grateful that we met later in life, rather than not at all. Much love to Joan, David, my nephews AJ and Joel, my nieces, Jeneane and Laura, and their spouses and extended families, who I finally was able to meet after so many years.

Table of Contents

SECTION 5: COMMONLY MISSPELLED WORDS

SECTION 6: MODERN GRAMMAR AND STYLE

SECTION 7: QUIZ ANSWERS

What This Grammar Workbook Can Do for You

The Elements of Style was written in 1918 by William Strunk Jr., an English professor at Cornell University. It was a modest, 38-page handout listing basic grammar rules, which Strunk distributed to students in his English classes. He probably never imagined that his primer would be widely read a century later; but it has helped generations of students and writers learn the basics of English grammar and remains popular today. It was hailed as "one of the 100 most influential books written in English" by Time magazine in 2011, and author Stephen King recommended it as must reading for all aspiring writers.

Down through the years, many versions of *The Elements of Style* have been published. Most are reproductions of Strunk's first edition, which is now in the public domain; but three versions are noteworthy to us in this workbook. If you are studying *The Elements of Style* for a college course, it is likely that you are reading one of these three editions:

1. Strunk's original work, written in 1918 and published privately in 1919. It is now in the public domain and widely available as a free e-book. We'll refer to it as "Strunk's first edition" in this workbook.

2. Macmillan Publishing commissioned editor E.B. White to compile an update to Strunk's book in 1959. A second update was published in 1972, a third in 1979, and a fourth in 2000. These versions are widely used in classrooms, and we collectively refer to them as the "Strunk & White edition." (ISBN 978-0205309023, paperback)

3. A 100-year anniversary edition was compiled by the editor of this workbook and published in 2017 as a tribute to Strunk's classic. It offers a variety of enhancements, including editor's notes on obsolete grammar rules, emojis to make sorting through correct and incorrect examples easier; and a study guide. An update published in 2018 features a new Introduction covering the nine parts of speech, and two new chapters on *Basic Rules of Capitalization* and *Style Rules for Better Writing*. We refer to it as the "2018 Classic Edition" (see right-hand column on next page for details).

Readers of all three versions of *The Elements of Style* can use this workbook to assess their mastery of the basic rules of English grammar. It contains 625 questions, divided into 27 quizzes with multiple-choice answers. Some quizzes apply to all three versions of Strunk's book; others are intended for readers of a particular edition. So, whatever version you are reading, you'll be able to benefit from the quiz modules in this book.

This grammar workbook has an interactive component, giving readers free online access to a virtual classroom devoted to *The Elements of Style*. This e-learning environment, hosted on the Virtual University website, offers a variety of features, including:

--Interactive multiple-choice quizzes with randomized questions and real-time scoring to help readers memorize and test their knowledge of essential grammar rules.

--A Web Resources section with curated videos and Web-based study materials to help readers learn English grammar.

--An expanded Vocabulary Guide listing 100+ grammar terms and definitions.

To access this virtual classroom, browse to: https://books.vu.org/titles/eos_grammar

Returning our focus to this workbook, it is unlikely that you will complete all 27 quiz units in a single day or that you would even want to attempt it. Instead, to derive the most benefit from this workbook, you should try to complete a few quizzes each day. Make sure that you have a firm grasp of the underlying grammar principles before going on to the next quiz. You will know that you are ready to proceed when you are able to answer all of the questions on the current quiz correctly.

Strunk's goal in writing his classic primer was to help students learn how to write grammatically correct prose. His book gives students and writers a blueprint they can follow to express their thoughts and ideas clearly, concisely, and effectively. Whether you are taking a college course and *The Elements of Style* is required reading, or you are a writer looking to polish your grammar and style, this workbook can help you to memorize and master the basic rules of English grammar outlined in Strunk's book and use that knowledge to make all of your writing exemplary.

Richard De A'Morelli, Editor
August, 2020

The Elements of Style: Classic Edition (2018)

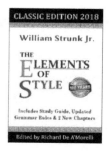

William Strunk Jr.
Editor, Richard De A'Morelli

This updated Classic Edition contains the original version of William Strunk's grammar primer, *The Elements of Style,* plus a variety of enhancements to make this book even more helpful. It is now used as a textbook in classes at University of Minnesota, Texas A&M University of Florida, UC Berkeley, and elsewhere.

Generations of college students and writers have learned the basics of English grammar from this short book. Strunk's original edition was rated "one of the 100 most influential books written in English" by Time in 2011, and iconic author Stephen King recommended it as a grammar primer that all aspiring writers should read. Many of Strunk's grammar rules still apply today; but the English language has changed over the past 100 years, and some rules are now obsolete. This 2018 update gives students and writers a blueprint they can follow to write clearly and effectively, using the essential rules of English Grammar. It offers the following enhancements:

1. Two new chapters have been added on Capitalization and Style Rules for Better Writing.

2. Editor's notes have been inserted to flag obsolete grammar rules and to provide up-to-date advice for students and writers.

3. Emojis are used throughout the book to help readers identify correct examples from errors at a glance.

4. A Study Guide is included, and the paperback edition provides blank, lined pages in the back of the book for note-taking.

ISBN #	Edition
978-1-643990-01-9	Kindle e-book (MOBI)
978-1-643990-00-2	Paperback (Amazon)
978-1-643990-03-3	Paperback (Ingram)
978-1-643990-04-0	Hardcover (Ingram)
978-1-643990-02-6	Nook/iStore e-book

Section 1
Elementary Rules of Usage

Quiz #1
Possessive Apostrophes

1.01. With a few exceptions, you should form the possessive singular of nouns by adding:

a) apostrophe + s (Bob's notebook)
b) apostrophe + es (James'es car)
c) s + apostrophe (Carls' book)

1.02. Consider the use of possessive apostrophes in these phrases. Which form is written incorrectly?

a) Charles's friend
b) the witch's malice
c) Ross'es poems
d) Carlos's house

1.03. You should use only an apostrophe and no "s" when writing the possessive form of Jesus, as in *Jesus' teachings*.

a) True
b) False

1.04. Consider the use of the possessive apostrophes in these phrases. Which phrase is written incorrectly?

a) Jesus' robe
b) Moses's teachings
c) Achilles' heel
d) Noah's ark

1.05. Which sentence is written correctly?

a) The cat licked *its* paw.
b) The cat licked *it's* paw.
c) The cat licked *its'* paw.
d) The cat licked *its's* paw.

1.06. Proper grammar might sometimes dictate that you use an apostrophe with the pronominal possessives *hers, theirs, yours,* and *oneself.*

a) True
b) False

1.07. Which phrase is written incorrectly?

a) Charles's friend
b) Donald's speech
c) The witchs' malice
d) Marcus's car

1.08. Which sentence is written correctly?

a) The hat is *hers'*.
b) The hat is *her's*.
c) The hat is *hers*.

1.09. Which phrase is written correctly?

a) Achilles's heel
b) Jesus' robe
c) Moses teachings
d) Noahs' ark

1.10. Which phrase is written incorrectly?

a) for conscience' sake
b) Isis's temple
c) Moses' laws

1.11. An apostrophe is required after the pronominal possessive *its.*

a) True
b) False

1.12. Consider the use of the possessive apostrophes in these sentences. Which sentence is written correctly?

a) They believe the land is *their's*, but they are wrong.
b) They believe the land is *there's*, but they are wrong.
c) They believe the land is *theirs'*, but they are wrong.
d) They believe the land is *theirs*, but they are wrong.

1.13. Which sentence is written correctly?

a) The choice is *yours'*, so decide quickly.
b) The choice is *yours*, so decide quickly.
c) The choice is *your's*, so decide quickly.

Quiz #2
Serial Commas

2.01. A comma placed before a conjunction in a series of three or more terms is called _____.

a) an Oxnard comma
b) a cereal comma
c) a parallel comma
d) a Harvard comma
e) None of these answers are correct.

2.02. In business firm names, you should omit the last comma in a series of names, as *Brown, Shipley & Co.*

a) True
b) False

2.03. Consider the use of commas in the following business name, where Joe Allen, Kelsey Jones, and Brad Smith are the owners. Which form is written correctly?

a) Allen, Jones, Smith, & Co.
b) Allen Jones, Smith & Co.
c) Allen, Jones, Smith & Co.
d) None of these answers are correct.
e) All of these answers are correct.

2.04. Which phrase uses a serial comma correctly?

a) red, white and blue
b) red, white, and blue
c) red, white and, blue
d) red, white, and, blue
e) None of these answers are correct.

2.05. Another name for a serial comma is _____.

a) an Oxford comma
b) a conjunctive comma
c) a relative comma
d) a parallel comma

2.06. Assume that the use of serial commas is required in your writing. Which phrase is written correctly?

a) gold, silver or copper
b) gold, silver or, copper
c) gold silver, or copper
d) gold, silver, or copper

2.07. Which sentence uses the serial comma correctly?

a) He opened the letter, read it, and discarded it.
b) He opened the letter, read it and discarded it.
c) He opened the letter, read it and, discarded it.

2.08. Which sentence uses the serial comma correctly?

a) Mary packed a turkey sandwich, one orange, two apples, and a cookie, in her son's lunch pail.
b) Mary packed a turkey sandwich, one orange, two apples and a cookie in her son's lunch pail.
c) Mary packed a turkey sandwich, one orange, two apples, and a cookie in her son's lunch pail.
d) Mary packed a turkey sandwich, one orange, two apples and a cookie, in her son's lunch pail.

Quiz #3
Parenthetical Expressions

3.01. Parenthetical expressions usually should be set off by commas.

a) True

b) False

3.02. Which sentence uses commas correctly to mark off a parenthetical phrase?

a) Sheila's husband, Captain Garcia paid us a visit today.

b) Sheila's husband Captain Garcia, paid us a visit today.

c) Sheila's husband, Captain Garcia, paid us a visit today.

d) Sheila's husband Captain Garcia paid us a visit today.

3.03. Read this sentence and choose the answer that best defines the italicized words: "The best way to see a country, *unless you are pressed for time*, is to travel on foot."

a) an appositive phrase

b) a conjunctive phrase

c) an inserted footnote

d) a parenthetical phrase

3.04. Which of these sentences uses commas correctly to mark off a parenthetical phrase?

a) My father, I am happy to say, has now fully recovered.

b) My father, I am happy to say has now fully recovered.

c) My father I am happy to say, has now fully recovered.

d) My father I am happy to say has now fully recovered.

3.05. Sometimes it is hard to decide whether a single word, such as "however," or a brief phrase, is or is not parenthetical.

a) True

b) False

3.06. With a parenthetical phrase, if the interruption to the flow of the sentence is slight, it is acceptable to omit the offsetting commas.

a) True

b) False

3.07. When a parenthetical expression is preceded by a conjunction, you should _____.

a) Write the first comma after the conjunction.

b) Write the first comma before the conjunction.

c) Omit the first comma if it looks strange.

d) Include a comma before and after the conjunction.

3.08. In a sentence with a parenthetical phrase, it is acceptable to insert the opening comma, and omit the closing comma, if it improves the flow of the passage.

a) True

b) False

3.09. These sentences contain a parenthetical phrase. Which sentence is written correctly?

a) He saw us coming and, unaware that we had learned of his treachery, greeted us with a smile.

b) He saw us coming and unaware that we had learned of his treachery, greeted us with a smile.

c) He saw us coming, and unaware that we had learned of his treachery, greeted us with a smile.

d) None of these constructions are written correctly.

3.10. A parenthetical expression is a clause or phrase that is inserted within another clause or phrase.

a) True

b) False

3.11. If a sentence contains a parenthetical phrase, and you delete that phrase, you will no longer have a complete sentence.

a) True
b) False

3.12. Consider the parenthetical phrase in these sentences. Which is written correctly?

a) The candidate, who best meets these requirements, will be hired for the job.
b) The candidate who best meets these requirements, will be hired for the job.
c) The candidate who best meets these requirements will be hired for the job.

3.13. Which phrase is punctuated correctly?

a) February to July 2016
b) February, to July, 2016
c) February, to July 2016
d) February to July, 2016

3.14. Which date is punctuated correctly?

a) April 6 2017
b) April 6, 2017
c) April, 6, 2017

3.15. Which date is punctuated correctly?

a) Monday, November 11, 2018
b) Monday, November 11 2018
c) Monday November 11, 2018
d) Monday November 11 2018

3.16. These sentences contain a parenthetical expression. Which is written correctly?

a) The day will come, when you will admit your mistake.
b) The day will come, when you will admit, your mistake.
c) The day will come when you will, admit your mistake.
d) The day will come when you will admit your mistake.

Quiz #4
Comma Usage in Clauses

4.01. A comma should be placed before a conjunction that introduces a coordinate clause.

a) True
b) False

4.02. In these sentences, a conjunction introduces a coordinate clause requiring a comma. Which sentence is written correctly?

a) The early records of the city have disappeared and the story of its first years can no longer be reconstructed.
b) The early records of the city have disappeared, and the story of its first years can no longer be reconstructed.
c) The early records of the city have disappeared, and the story of its first years, can no longer be reconstructed.

4.03. Two-part sentences of which the second member is introduced by *as* (in the sense of *because*), *for*, *or*, *nor*, and *while* (in the sense of *and at the same time*) require a comma after the conjunction.

a) True
b) False

4.04. Strunk advises that it is not necessarily good style to make all your sentences short and brief. An occasional loose sentence prevents your style from becoming too formal and gives the reader a bit of relief.

a) True
b) False

4.05. If a dependent clause, or an introductory phrase that must be set off by a comma, precedes a second independent clause, a comma is required after the conjunction.

a) True
b) False

4.06. In these constructions, a conjunction introduces a coordinate clause. Which sentence is written correctly?

a) The situation at the coal mine is perilous but there is still one chance of escape.

b) The situation at the coal mine is perilous, but there is still, one chance of escape.

c) The situation at the coal mine is perilous, but there is still one chance of escape.

d) The situation at the coal mine is perilous but, there is still one chance of escape.

4.07. Which sentence is punctuated correctly?

a) The situation is perilous, but if we are prepared to act promptly we may still escape.

b) The situation is perilous, but if we are prepared to act promptly; we may still escape.

c) The situation is perilous; but if we are prepared to act promptly we may still escape.

d) The situation is perilous, but if we are prepared to act promptly, we may still escape.

4.08. In a two-part sentence, if the second member is introduced by an adverb, you should use a semicolon rather than a comma to connect the two parts.

a) True

b) False

4.09. In these constructions, the subject is the same for both clauses and is expressed only once. Which is written correctly?

a) I have heard his arguments but am still unconvinced.

b) I have heard his arguments, but am still unconvinced.

c) I have heard his arguments; but am still unconvinced.

d) I have heard his arguments but am, still unconvinced.

4.10. In the following sentences, the subject is the same for both clauses and is expressed only once. Which sentence is written correctly?

a) He has had several years' experience, and is thoroughly competent.

b) He has had several years' experience; and is thoroughly competent.

c) He has had several years' experience and is thoroughly competent.

d) He has had several years' experience and, is thoroughly competent.

4.11. The connectives *so* and *yet* may be used either as adverbs or as conjunctions, where the second clause is intended to be coordinate or subordinate; so, using either a comma or a semicolon may be appropriate.

a) True

b) False

4.12. When the subject is the same for both clauses and is expressed only once, a comma is not required if the connective is *but*.

a) True

b) False

4.13. When the subject is the same for both clauses and is expressed only once, if the connective is *and*, you should omit the comma if the relation between the two statements is close or immediate.

a) True

b) False

Quiz #5
Compound Sentences

5.01. It is acceptable to break a compound sentence into two shorter elements, where both form complete sentences, but doing so often results in choppy wording.

a) True
b) False

5.02. You may break sentences in two when one element or the other does not form a complete sentence, as long as you mark the break with a period, as in this example: "I met Kate on a cruise in June. Sailing from San Diego to Cancun."

a) True
b) False

5.03. Which sentence is punctuated correctly?

a) I met Kate on a cruise last year ago. Sailing from San Diego to Cancun.
b) I met Kate on a cruise last year, sailing from San Diego to Cancun.
c) I met Kate on a cruise last year: sailing from San Diego to Cancun.
d) None of these sentences are punctuated correctly.

5.04. It is acceptable to make an emphatic word or expression serve the purpose of a sentence and to punctuate it accordingly, as: "Again and again he called out. No reply."

a) True
b) False

Quiz #6
Semicolons in Compound Sentences

6.01. If two or more clauses, grammatically complete and not joined by a conjunction, are written to form a compound sentence, the proper punctuation mark is a semicolon.

a) True
b) False

6.02. The following sentences contain two complete clauses not joined by a conjunction. Which sentence is written incorrectly?

a) Stevenson's romances are entertaining; they are full of exciting adventures.
b) Stevenson's romances are entertaining. They are full of exciting adventures.
c) Stevenson's romances are entertaining, they are full of exciting adventures.
d) All of these answers are incorrect.

6.03. The following sentences contain two complete clauses joined by a conjunction. Which sentence is written correctly?

a) Stevenson's romances are entertaining, for they are full of exciting adventures.
b) Stevenson's romances are entertaining. For they are full of exciting adventures.
c) Stevenson's romances are entertaining; for they are full of exciting adventures.
d) All of these sentences are written correctly.

6.04. If the second clause in a sentence containing two complete clauses is preceded by an adverb, such as *accordingly, besides, then, therefore,* or *thus,* and not by a conjunction, the semicolon is not required.

a) True
b) False

6.05. The following sentences contain two complete clauses not joined by a conjunction. Which sentence is not written correctly?

a) It is half past five; we can't reach town before dark.

b) It is half past five; and we can't reach town before dark.

c) It is half past five. We can't reach town before dark.

d) All of these sentences are written correctly.

6.06. If a conjunction is inserted between two complete clauses rather than a semicolon, the correct punctuation mark to use is a _____.

a) comma

b) semicolon

c) period

d) ellipsis

6.07. These sentences contain two complete clauses joined by a conjunction. Which is not written correctly?

a) It is nearly half past five, and we cannot reach town before the sun goes down.

b) It is nearly half past five; we cannot reach town before the sun goes down.

c) It is nearly half past five, we cannot reach town before the sun goes down.

d) All of these sentences are written correctly.

6.08. Which sentence is written correctly?

a) Man proposes; God disposes.

b) The car stopped, the driver fled, the police pursued.

c) The summer was exceedingly hot and dry, and, wildfires ravaged the northern part of the state.

d) None of these sentences are written correctly.

6.09. If a sentence consists of two complete clauses, and the two are very short and alike in form, it is usually acceptable to use a comma, as, "Anya complains, Lorena acts."

a) True

b) False

6.10. Which sentence is written correctly?

a) The door swung open, the gun fired; the intruder fled.

b) The door swung open, the gun fired: the intruder fled.

c) The door swung open, the gun fired, the intruder fled.

d) None of these are written correctly.

Quiz #7

Participial Phrases

7.01. A participial phrase at the beginning of a sentence may refer to the grammatical subject or to any other noun in the sentence.

a) True

b) False

7.02. Participial phrases preceded by a conjunction or a preposition, nouns in apposition, adjectives, and adjective phrases must always refer to the grammatical subject if they begin the sentence.

a) True

b) False

7.03. Which construction is grammatically preferable?

a) On arriving in Chicago, David's friends met him at the station.

b) When he arrived in Chicago, David's friends met him at the station.

c) Upon his arrival at the station, in Chicago, David's friends met him.

7.04. Which construction is grammatically preferable?

a) A courageous soldier, Capt. Jones was entrusted with the defense of the city.

b) The entrusted Capt. Jones, a courageous soldier, with the defense of the city.

c) A courageous soldier, the defense of the city was entrusted to Capt. Jones.

7.05. Which sentence is written correctly?

a) Young and inexperienced, the task seemed easy to me.

b) The task seemed easy to me, young and inexperienced.

c) Young and inexperienced, I thought the task easy.

d) None of these forms are correct.

7.06. Which form is grammatically preferable?

a) Without a friend to counsel him, the temptation for him proved irresistible.

b) Without a friend to counsel him, the temptation he found was irresistible.

c) Without a friend to counsel him, he found the temptation irresistible.

7.07. Which sentence is written correctly?

a) Being in a dilapidated condition, the house was for sale very cheap.

b) Being in a dilapidated condition, I was able to buy the house very cheap.

c) I bought the house very cheap, being in a dilapidated condition.

7.08. Which sentence is written correctly?

a) Wondering in dismay what to do next, the clock struck twelve.

b) Wondering in dismay what to do next, I heard the clock strike twelve.

c) Wondering what to do next in dismay, the clock struck twelve.

Section 2
Basic Composition Principles

Quiz #8
Paragraphs in Composition

8.01. A paragraph should be the basic unit of composition, and each paragraph should express a complete thought.

a) True

b) False

8.02. If the subject on which you are writing is of a trivial nature, or if you intend to treat it very briefly, you should still subdivide it into multiple paragraphs, and some of those paragraphs may consist of just one sentence.

a) True

b) False

8.03. For a subject that is complex and consists of several or more topics, it is acceptable to combine multiple topics into a single paragraph to save space and help readers move through your writing quickly.

a) True

b) False

8.04. The beginning of each paragraph is a signal to the reader that _____.

a) The writer has lost track of his topic and needs another paragraph to clarify the point he is trying to make.

b) A new idea is being introduced that is not directly related to the preceding paragraph.

c) A new step in the development of the subject has been reached.

d) All of these answers are correct.

8.05. A brief description, a brief book review or account of a single incident, a narrative that merely outlines an action, the expressing of a single idea, any one of these is best written in a single paragraph.

a) True

b) False

8.06. A report on a poem, written for a literature class, might typically consist of just one paragraph.

a) True

b) False

8.07. A single sentence, with a few exceptions, should not be written as a paragraph.

a) True

b) False

8.08. For sentences of transition, and in textbooks, guides, and other works in which many topics are treated briefly, it is not acceptable to write a single sentence as a paragraph.

a) True

b) False

8.09. In dialogue, each speech, even if only a single word, is a paragraph by itself. In other words, a new paragraph begins with each change of speaker.

a) True

b) False

Quiz #9
Topic Sentences in Paragraphs

9.01. Beginning each paragraph with a topic sentence will allow readers to discover the purpose of each paragraph as they begin to read it, and to retain this purpose in mind as they end it.

a) True
b) False

9.02. In a well-structured paragraph, the topic sentence comes at or near the beginning; the succeeding sentences either emphasize the thought of the topic sentence or state some important consequence; and the final sentence explains, establishes, or develops the statement made in the topic sentence.

a) True
b) False

9.03. You should avoid ending a paragraph with an unimportant detail or a digression.

a) True
b) False

9.04. If a paragraph forms part of a larger composition, its relation to what precedes, or its function as a part of the whole, may need to be expressed. This can be done sometimes by a mere word or phrase (*again; therefore*; *for the same reason*) in the topic sentence.

a) True
b) False

Quiz #10
Active Voice

10.01. The active voice is usually more direct and vigorous than the passive voice.

a) True
b) False

10.02. Which sentence is written in active voice?

a) I shall always remember my first visit to Paris.
b) My first visit to Paris will always be remembered by me.

10.03. Although writing in active voice should be heavily favored, sometimes a sentence will read better if written in passive voice, or using passive voice may even be necessary.

a) True
b) False

10.04. Which construction is grammatically preferable in a paragraph discussing the dramatists of the Restoration?

a) Modern readers have little esteem for the dramatists of the Restoration.
b) The dramatists of the Restoration are little esteemed today.

10.05. Which construction is grammatically preferable in a paragraph discussing the tastes of modern readers?

a) The dramatists of the Restoration are little esteemed by modern readers today.
b) Modern readers have little esteem for the dramatists of the Restoration.

10.06. As a rule, your prose will be clearer and more concrete if you favor constructions in which one passive depends directly upon another.

a) True
b) False

10.07. If your aim is to avoid making one passive depend directly on another, which construction should you use?

a) He has been proved to have been seen entering the room.

b) It has been proved that he was seen entering the room.

10.08. A common fault is to use as the subject of a passive construction a noun that expresses the entire action and leaves to the verb no function other than completing the sentence.

a) True

b) False

10.09. Which construction contains a grammar fault that should be avoided?

a) Confirmation of these reports cannot be obtained.

b) These reports cannot be confirmed.

10.10. Which sentence avoids passive construction of a noun that expresses the entire action and leaves the verb with no function other than completing the sentence?

a) A survey of this region was made in 1900.

b) This region was surveyed in 1900.

10.11. Which sentence avoids passive construction of a noun that expresses the entire action and leaves the verb with no function other than completing the sentence?

a) Mobilization of the army was rapidly effected.

b) The army was rapidly mobilized.

10.12. Many bland descriptive sentences can be made lively and more emphatic by substituting a verb in the active voice for some such perfunctory expression as *there is*, or *could be heard*.

a) True

b) False

10.13. The habitual use of passive voice makes for forcible writing. This is true not only in narrative mainly concerned with action, but in writing of any kind.

a) True

b) False

10.14. Which sentence substitutes a verb in the active voice to make the passage interesting or emphatic?

a) The sound of a guitar somewhere in the house could be heard.

b) In the house somewhere, the sounds of a guitar were heard.

c) Somewhere in the house a guitar hummed sleepily.

10.15. Which sentence substitutes a verb in the active voice to make the passage interesting or emphatic?

a) There were a great number of dead leaves lying on the ground.

b) On the ground were a great number of dead leaves.

c) Dead leaves covered the ground.

10.16. Which construction is grammatically preferable?

a) The reason that he left college was that his health became impaired.

b) Failing health compelled him to leave college.

Quiz #11
Writing in Positive Form

11.01. You should avoid tame, colorless, non-committal language, and make definite assertions in your writing.

a) True
b) False

11.02. The word *not* is inherently weak. Consciously or unconsciously, the reader is dissatisfied with being told only what is not; he wishes to be told what is. Therefore, as a rule, it is better to express even a negative in positive form.

a) True
b) False

11.03. Which sentence is grammatically better?

a) He was not very often on time.
b) He usually came late.

11.04. Which sentence is written correctly?

a) He thought the study of Latin useless.
b) He did not think that studying Latin was much use.

11.05. Which construction is stronger?

a) Not honest
b) Dishonest

11.06. Strunk advises that you should use *not* as a means of denial or evasion, and never in antithesis.

a) True
b) False

11.07. Which passage adheres to Strunk's grammar rules more effectively?

a) *The Taming of the Shrew* is rather weak in spots. Shakespeare does not portray Katharine as a very admirable character, nor does Bianca remain long in memory as an important character in Shakespeare's works.

b) The women in *The Taming of the Shrew* are unattractive. Katharine is disagreeable, Bianca insignificant.

11.08. Negative words other than *not* are usually strong.

a) True
b) False

11.09. Which construction is weaker?

a) Did not remember
b) Forgot

11.10. Which construction is stronger?

a) Did not have much confidence in
b) Distrusted

Quiz #12
Definite, Specific, Concrete Language

12.01. A writer is well advised to prefer the specific to the general, the definite to the vague, the concrete to the abstract.

a) True
b) False

12.02. Which construction is more definite and specific?

a) A period of unfavorable weather set in.
b) It rained every day for a week.

12.03. Which construction is more definite and specific?

a) He grinned as he pocketed the coin.
b) He showed satisfaction as he took possession of his well-earned reward.

12.04. Prose, in particular narrative and descriptive prose, is made vivid by definite and concrete words that evoke mental pictures in the reader's mind.

a) True
b) False

12.05. Which construction is more definite and specific?

a) There is a general agreement among those who have enjoyed the experience that surf riding is productive of great exhilaration.
b) All who have tried surf riding agree that it is most exhilarating.

Quiz #13
Trimming Unnecessary Words

13.01. If you want to write lively and exemplary prose, you should make all your sentences short, use simple words, and make every word tell.

a) True
b) False

13.02. Which sentence should be rewritten to eliminate word clutter?

a) Because Marcus failed to pay his bill, his electricity was shut off.
b) Marcus failed to pay his bill, so his electricity was shut off.
c) Owing to the fact that Marcus failed to pay his bill, his electricity was shut off.
d) All of these sentences should be rewritten to eliminate word clutter.

13.03. Prof. Strunk advises that vigorous writing is concise, and a sentence should contain no unnecessary words, a paragraph no unnecessary sentences.

a) True
b) False

13.04. Which expression is less concise?

a) The question as to whether
b) Whether

13.05. Which expression is more concise?

a) There is no doubt but that
b) No doubt

13.06. Which construction contains word clutter?

a) Used for fuel
b) Used for fuel purposes

13.07. Which expression is more concise?

a) He
b) He is a man who

13.08. Which sentence should be rewritten to eliminate word clutter?

a) Though I left early, I was still late for my appointment.

b) In spite of the fact that I left early, I was still late for my appointment.

c) Although I left early, I was still late for my appointment.

13.09. Which phrase is less concise?

a) In a hasty manner

b) Hastily

13.10. Which phrase is more concise?

a) This is a subject which

b) This subject

13.11. Which sentence is free of word clutter?

a) His story is strange.

b) His story is a strange one.

13.12. The expression *the fact that* should be deleted from every sentence in which it occurs.

a) True

b) False

13.13. Which sentence should be rewritten to avoid word clutter?

a) We call your attention to the fact that your taxes are delinquent.

b) We remind you that your taxes are delinquent.

c) We are notifying you that your taxes are delinquent.

13.14. Which construction is grammatically preferable?

a) The fact that he had not succeeded on the first attempt simply inspired him to try harder.

b) His failure on the first attempt simply inspired him to try harder.

13.15. *Who is, which was,* and the like are often superfluous and should be written out of sentences.

a) True

b) False

13.16. Which sentence should be rewritten to avoid word clutter?

a) I was unaware that Ariana was born in Italy.

b) I was unaware of the fact that Ariana was born in Italy.

c) I did not know that Ariana was born in Italy.

13.17. Which of these sentences reflect better grammar?

a) The fact that I had arrived two hours late was cause for concern.

b) My arrival two hours late was cause for concern.

13.18. Which construction is more concise?

a) His brother, a member of the same firm

b) His brother, who is a member of the same firm

13.19. Which construction is grammatically preferable?

a) Trafalgar, which was Nelson's last battle

b) Trafalgar, Nelson's last battle

13.20. A common violation of conciseness is presenting a single complex idea, step by step, in a series of sentences or independent clauses that might be more effectively combined into one.

a) True

b) False

Quiz #14
Loose Sentences in Succession

14.01. A "loose" sentence is a particular type consisting of two coordinate clauses, the second introduced by a conjunction or relative.

a) True
b) False

14.02. A series of loose sentences might be acceptable in writing but will likely become monotonous.

a) True
b) False

14.03. If you find that you've written a series of loose sentences, you should:

a) Leave that paragraph as is, but make sure that the sentences in the next paragraph are varied.
b) Recast at least enough of them to remove the monotony.
c) Include a footnote to the reader that your writing in this section of your document is choppy, but this style is necessary in the current paragraph.
d) None of these answers are correct.

Quiz #15
Expressing Coordinate Ideas

15.01. The principle of "parallel construction" requires that expressions of similar content and function should be outwardly similar.

a) True
b) False

15.02. Which phrase expresses coordinate ideas correctly?

a) The French, the Italians, Spanish, and Greeks
b) The French, the Italians, the Spanish, and the Greeks
c) The French, Italians, Spanish, and the Greeks.

15.03. Which sentence is written correctly?

a) Formerly, science was taught by the text-book method, while now the laboratory method is employed.
b) Formerly, science was taught by the text-book method; now it is taught by the laboratory method.
c) Neither sentence is written correctly.

15.04. An article or a preposition that applies to all the members of a series must either be used only before the first term or else be repeated before each term.

a) True
b) False

15.05. The expressions *both, and; not, but; not only, but also; either, or; first, second, third*; and the like are called:

a) Prepositional expressions
b) Conjunctive clauses
c) Correlative expressions
d) Coordinated clauses

15.06. Which sentence is written incorrectly because it relies on unlike constructions?

a) The ceremony was both long and tedious.
b) It was both a long ceremony and very tedious.

15.07. Correlative expressions should be followed by the same grammatical construction, that is, by the same part of speech, such as "both Aisha and I" and "not silk, but a cheap substitute."

a) True
b) False

15.08. Which construction is grammatically incorrect?

a) In spring, summer, and in winter
b) In spring, summer, and winter
c) In spring, in summer, and in winter

15.09. Which sentence is flawed because it relies on unlike constructions?

a) My objections are, first, the injustice of the measure; second, that it is unconstitutional.

b) My objections are, first, that the measure is unjust; second, that it is unconstitutional.

15.10. Which sentence is written correctly?

a) A time not for words, but for action.
b) A time not for words, but action.

15.11. Which sentence is written incorrectly?

a) You must either grant his request or incur his ill will.

b) Either you must grant his request or incur his ill will.

Quiz #16
Keep Related Words Together

16.01. In a sentence, you should try to bring together the words, and groups of words, that are related in thought, and keep apart those which are not so related.

a) True
b) False

16.02. According to modern grammar rules, it is often acceptable to start a sentence with "There is" or a similar form of the expression.

a) True
b) False

16.03. Modifiers should come, if possible, next to the word they modify.

a) True
b) False

16.04. Which of these sentences reflects better grammar?

a) Wordsworth, in the fifth book of *The Excursion*, gives a minute description of this church.

b) In the fifth book of *The Excursion*, Wordsworth gives a minute description of this church.

16.05. Which construction reflects better grammar?

a) Cast iron, when treated in a Bessemer converter, is changed into steel.

b) By treatment in a Bessemer converter, cast iron is changed into steel.

16.06. Usually, a relative pronoun should come immediately _____.

a) before its antecedent
b) before a preposition
c) after its antecedent
d) after a predicate

16.07. Which form is grammatically preferable?

a) He wrote three articles about his adventures in Spain, which were published in *Harper's Magazine*.

b) He published in *Harper's Magazine* three articles about his adventures in Spain.

16.08. Which passage is written correctly?

a) This is a portrait of Benjamin Harrison, grandson of William Henry Harrison. He became President in 1889.

b) This is a portrait of Benjamin Harrison, grandson of William Henry Harrison, who became President in 1889.

16.09. Which sentence is less ambiguous?

a) He found only two mistakes.

b) He only found two mistakes.

16.10. Which sentence is preferable?

a) There was a look in his eye that boded mischief.

b) In his eye was a look that boded mischief.

16.11. A noun in apposition should never come between antecedent and relative, because in such a combination ambiguity can arise.

a) True

b) False

16.12. If several expressions modify the same word, they should be so arranged to avoid ambiguity or confusing the reader.

a) True

b) False

16.13. Which passage is less ambiguous?

a) On Tuesday at eight P. M., Major R. E. Joyce will give in Bailey Hall a lecture on "My Experiences in Mesopotamia." The public is invited.

b) Major R. E. Joyce will give a lecture on Tuesday evening in Bailey Hall, to which the public is invited, on "My Experiences in Mesopotamia" at eight P. M.

16.14. Which sentence is less ambiguous?

a) All the members were not present.

b) Not all the members were present.

Quiz #17
Keeping to One Tense in Summaries

17.01. In summarizing a poem, story, or novel, you should use the past tense, since the poem was written in the past, though you may use present tense if you prefer.

a) True

b) False

17.02. Prof. Strunk advises that in summarizing the action of a drama, you should always use the _____.

a) past tense

b) future tense

c) present tense

d) future perfect tense

17.03. As a general rule, it is good practice to shift from one tense to another in your writing, as it gives your prose a sense of being fresh, and it will hold your reader's interest.

a) True

b) False

17.04. In writing a summary, you should aim to write an orderly discussion supported by evidence, not a summary with occasional comment.

a) True

b) False

17.05. In presenting the statements or the thought of someone else, as in summarizing an essay or reporting a speech, you should avoid intercalating such expressions as "he said," "he stated," "the speaker added," "the author also thinks," and the like.

a) True

b) False

17.06. When summarizing a poem, a story, or a novel, whichever tense is used in the summary, a past tense in indirect discourse or in indirect question should be changed to present tense.

a) True

b) False

17.07. In newspapers and in many kinds of textbooks, summaries of one kind or another may be indispensable, and it is a useful exercise for children in primary schools to retell a story in their own words. But in the criticism or interpretation of literature, you should be careful to avoid dropping into summary.

a) True

b) False

Quiz #18
Placing Emphatic Words in a Sentence

18.01. The proper place in a sentence for the word, or group of words, which you want to make most prominent is usually _____.

a) the end
b) the beginning
c) the middle
d) wherever it sounds best

18.02. Which sentence better emphasizes the thought that the writer is trying to establish as the most prominent?

a) Humanity has hardly advanced in fortitude since that time, though it has advanced in many other ways.
b) Humanity, since that time, has advanced in many other ways, but it has hardly advanced in fortitude.

18.03. Besides the end of a sentence, the other prominent position in a sentence is the beginning, and any element in the sentence, other than the subject, may become emphatic when placed first.

a) True
b) False

18.04. The word or group of words entitled to a position of prominence in a sentence is usually the logical predicate.

a) True
b) False

18.05. Which sentence better emphasizes the thought that the writer is trying to establish as the most prominent?

a) This steel is principally used for making razors, because of its hardness.
b) Because of its hardness, this steel is principally used in making razors.

18.06. The principle that the proper place for what is to be made most prominent is the end applies equally to the words of a sentence, to the sentences of a paragraph, and to the paragraphs of a composition.

a) True
b) False

Section 3
Matters of Form

Quiz #19
Headings and References

19.01. Prof. Strunk advises that you should leave a blank line after the title or heading of a manuscript, and on subsequent pages, you should...

a) leave a blank line and begin typing on the next line

b) type the title followed by a blank line on every page

c) begin typing on the first line

d) None of these answers are correct.

19.02. In a scholarly work requiring exact references, titles that occur frequently should be abbreviated and the full forms given in the index or in a preface at the beginning.

a) True

b) False

19.03. You should omit the words *act, scene, line, book, page, volume* in references to particular works, except when referring to only one of them.

a) True

b) False

19.04. As a general practice, you should give references in the body of the sentence, not in parenthesis or in footnotes.

a) True

b) False

Quiz #20
Quotations

20.01. Colloquialisms and slang do not require quotation marks, unless such marks would normally be required, such as to set off dialogue or a quoted excerpt.

a) True

b) False

20.02. Quotations introduced by the word *that* are regarded as indirect discourse and should be enclosed in quotation marks.

a) True

b) False

20.03. Consider the use of quotation marks and commas in these sentences. Which passage is written correctly?

a) I recall the maxim of La Rochefoucauld; "Gratitude is a lively sense of benefits to come."

b) I recall the maxim of La Rochefoucauld, ""Gratitude is a lively sense of benefits to come.""

c) I recall the maxim of La Rochefoucauld, "Gratitude is a lively sense of benefits to come."

d) None of these are sentences are correct.

20.04. Consider the use of quotation marks and commas in these sentences. Which passage is written correctly?

a) Aristotle says "Art is an imitation of nature."

b) Aristotle says, 'Art is an imitation of nature."

c) Aristotle says, Art is an imitation of nature.

d) Aristotle says, "Art is an imitation of nature."

20.05. Quotations grammatically in apposition, or the direct objects of verbs, should be preceded by a comma and enclosed in quotation marks.

a) True

b) False

20.06. Consider the indirect quotation in these passages. Which sentence is written correctly?

a) Keats declares that, "beauty is truth, truth beauty."

b) Keats declares that beauty is truth, truth beauty.

c) Keats declares that: beauty is truth, truth beauty.

d) Keats declares that "beauty is truth, truth beauty."

20.07. Proverbial expressions and familiar phrases of literary origin require quotation marks.

a) True

b) False

20.08. Consider the proverbial expression used in these constructions. Which sentence is written correctly?

a) "These are the times that try men's souls."

b) These are the "times" that "try men's souls."

c) "These are the times" that try men's souls.

d) These are the times that try men's souls.

e) None of these answers are correct.

20.09. Consider the phrase used in the following constructions. Which sentence is written correctly?

a) He lives far, from the madding crowd.

b) He lives far from "the madding crowd."

c) He lives far from the madding crowd.

Quiz #21
Hyphenation

This quiz on hyphenation is for readers of Strunk's first edition of *The Elements of* Style (including free and public domain versions) as well as the 2018 Classic Edition. Strunk & White's edition does not contain a chapter on hyphenation, so if you are reading that text, skip to the next chapter in this workbook.

The rules of hyphenation, like other rules of English grammar, are prone to change as time goes by. In Prof. Strunk's day, it was customary practice that if room exists at the end of a line for one or more syllables of a word but not for the whole word, the word should be divided on a syllable, unless this involves cutting off only a single letter, or cutting off only two letters of a long word. Modern style guides, however, often advise that a word should not be broken if fewer than three letters would remain on the current line or the subsequent line.

For this quiz, assume that Strunk's hyphenation rules apply and your objective is to properly break each word at the end of a line using a single hyphen, and not to hyphenate each syllable. Though multi-syllable words can be broken in several ways, only one answer is correct for each question.

21.01. How would you break *knowledge* at the end of a line?

a) know-ledge

b) knowl-edge

c) kno-wledge

21.02. How would you break *Shakespeare* at the end of a line?

a) Shakes-peare

b) Shak-espeare

c) Shake-speare

21.03. How would you break *describe* at the end of a line?

a) des-cribe

b) de-scribe

c) desc-ribe

21.04. How would you break *atmosphere* at the end of a line?

a) atmo-sphere

b) atmos-phere

c) atmosph-ere

21.05. Using Strunk's "divide on the vowel" rule, how would you break *edible* at the end of a line?

a) edi-ble

b) ed-ible

c) e-dible

21.06. Using Strunk's "divide on the vowel" rule, how would you break *proposition* at the end of a line?

a) propos-ition

b) prop-osition

c) propo-sition

21.07. How would you break *ordinary* at the end of a line?

a) ord-inary

b) ordi-nary

c) ordin-ary

21.08. How would you break *religious* at the end of a line?

a) reli-gious

b) relig-ious

c) rel-igious

21.09. How would you break *opponents* at the end of a line?

a) oppon-ents

b) opp-onents

c) oppo-nents

21.10. How would you break *regular* at the end of a line?

a) re-gular

b) regul-ar

c) regu-lar

21.11. How would you break *classification* at the end of a line?

a) class-ification

b) classi-fication

c) classif-ication

21.12. How would you break *decorative* at the end of a line?

a) deco-rative

b) I-ative

c) de-corative

21.13. How would you break *president* at the end of a line?

a) presi-dent

b) pre-sident

c) presid-ent

d) None of these answers are correct.

21.14. How would you break *Apennines* at the end of a line?

a) Ap-ennines

b) Apen-nines

c) Apenn-ines

21.15. How would you break *Cincinnati* at the end of a line?

a) Cincinn-ati

b) Cincin-nati

c) Cinci-nnati

d) None of these answers are correct.

21.16. How would you break *referring* at the end of a line?

a) refer-ring

b) 39yran-ing

c) ref-erring

21.17. How would you break *telling* at the end of a line?

a) te-lling

b) tell-ing

c) tel-ling

21.18. How would you break *fortune* at the end of a line?

a) fort-une

b) for-tune

c) fortu-ne

21.19. How would you break *picture* at the end of a line?

a) pic-ture

b) pict-ure

c) pictu-re

21.20. How would you break *single* at the end of a line?

a) sing-le

b) si-ngle

c) sin-gle

21.21. How would you break *illustration* at the end of a line?

a) illu-stration

b) illus-tration

c) illust-ration

d) illustrat-ion

21.22. How would you break *substantial* at the end of a line?

a) substant-ial

b) subs-tantial

c) substan-tial

21.23. How would you break *instruction* at the end of a line?

a) instruc-tion

b) instruct-ion

c) ins-truction

21.24. How would you break *suggestion* at the end of a line?

a) sugg-estion

b) suggest-ion

c) sugges-tion

21.25. How would you break *incendiary* at the end of a line?

a) incend-iary

b) incen-diary

c) incendia-ry

Section 4
Frequently Misused Words
and Expressions

Quiz #22
Misused Words & Expressions (Part 1)

This quiz module is for readers of Strunk's first edition of *The Elements of Style*, as well as the 2018 Classic Edition and the Strunk & White edition. Some of the questions in this section contain italicized text intended to direct your attention to specific expressions you should evaluate. Consider these italicized words to ascertain the correct answer for each question.

For more self-test questions on misused words and expressions, readers of Strunk's first edition and the 2018 Classic Edition should review Quiz #23; readers of the Strunk & White edition should review Quiz #24.

22.01. Which sentence is written correctly?

a) The patient says that she is feeling *alright* today.

b) The patient says that she is feeling *allright* today.

c) The patient says that she is feeling *all right* today.

d) None of these forms are written correctly.

22.02. The words *can* and *may* have the same meaning, and the two words may be used interchangeably.

a) True

b) False

22.03. Which phrase is written correctly?

a) I have no doubt but that...

b) I have no doubt that...

c) Both forms are written correctly.

22.04. Which construction is grammatically correct?

a) Many of the rooms were poorly ventilated.

b) In many cases, the rooms were poorly ventilated.

22.05. The following sentences compare the quality of one essay to another. Which sentence is grammatically flawed?

a) Laura's essay is as good as his, or better.

b) Laura's essay is as good or better than his.

c) Laura's essay is as good as his, if not better.

22.06. Which sentence is written correctly?

a) Whether the assassin is convicted will depend on the evidence presented.

b) As to whether the assassin is convicted will depend on the evidence presented.

22.07. Which phrase is written correctly?

a) He could not help seeing that...

b) He could not help see but that...

c) He could not help but see that...

22.08. Which sentence is written correctly?

a) It has rarely been the case that mistakes have been made.

b) Few mistakes have been made.

22.09. *Claim* is not a proper substitute for *declare, charge,* or *maintain.*

a) True

b) False

22.10. The word *certainly* is a good choice in a sentence where you want to intensify the point being made, just as the word *very* is a good choice to emphasize your point.

a) True

b) False

22.11. Which passage uses the word *but* more effectively?

a) America had vast resources, *but* she seemed wholly unprepared for war. *But* within a year she had created an army of four million men.

b) America seemed wholly unprepared for war, *but* she had vast resources. Within a year she had created an army of four million men.

22.12. Which sentence is written correctly?

a) I consider him as thoroughly competent.

b) I consider he is thoroughly competent.

c) I consider him thoroughly competent.

22.13. When Strunk wrote *The Elements of Style* in the early 1900s, his advice was to treat *data* as a plural noun. Today, *data* is widely used as both singular and plural.

a) True

b) False

22.14. Which sentence is written correctly?

a) The red Ford is *different among* the other cars on the lot.

b) The red Ford is *different than* the other cars on the lot.

c) The red Ford is *different from* the other cars on the lot.

22.15. Which sentence is written correctly?

a) He claimed to be the sole surviving heir.

b) He claimed that he was the sole surviving heir.

22.16. Which statement accurately describes the division of plays and poems?

a) Plays are *divided into* acts, but poems are *composed of* stanzas.

b) Plays are *composed of* acts, but poems are *divided into* stanzas.

c) Plays are *grouped into* acts, but poems are *grouped into* stanzas.

22.17. Which sentence describing Mario's carelessness is grammatically correct?

a) Mario lost the game *from* his own carelessness.

b) Mario lost the game *due to* his own carelessness.

c) Mario lost the game *because of* his own carelessness.

d) None of these sentences are correct.

22.18. It is appropriate to use the expression *due to* in some constructions, but not others. With that in mind, which sentence is written incorrectly?

a) This invention is *due to* Edison.

b) They suffered costly losses *due to* preventable fires.

c) Franco slipped and fell *due to* his own carelessness.

22.19. Prof. Strunk advises that *folk* is a collective noun, equivalent to *people*, and it denotes plural form.

a) True

b) False

22.20. Used as a noun, *affect* means "result," and as a verb, it means to "bring about, accomplish."

a) True

b) False

22.21. As a verb, *effect* means "to produce something or cause something to occur," and *affect* means "to influence."

a) True

b) False

22.22. Consider the use of *effect* and *affect* in these phrases and identify the grammatically flawed construction.

a) an Oriental *effect*

b) *effects* in pale green

c) broad *affects* can be seen

d) a charming *effect* was produced by

22.23. *Etc.* is equivalent to "and the rest," "and so forth." It typically follows a series of items in a list and indicates more items could have been listed.

a) True

b) False

22.24. You should never use *etc.* at the end of a list introduced by *such as, for example,* or any similar expression.

a) True

b) False

22.25. The words *less* and *fewer* mean the same and can be used interchangeably.

a) True

b) False

22.26. Which form reflects better grammar?

a) He is a man who is very ambitious.

b) He is very ambitious.

22.27. Sometimes *factor* is appropriate to use in a sentence; other times, it muddles the writer's point and should not be used. Which sentence reflects better grammar?

a) He won the match by being better trained.

b) His superior training was the great factor in his winning the match.

22.28. Which sentence is grammatically preferable?

a) Heavy artillery has become an increasingly important factor in deciding battles.

b) Heavy artillery has played a constantly larger part in deciding battles.

22.29. Which sentence contains flawed grammar that should never appear in academic or formal writing?

a) Those dogs have fleas from being outdoors.

b) Those dogs got fleas from being outdoors.

c) Those dogs have got fleas from being outdoors.

d) None of these sentences are incorrect.

22.30. Which sentence is grammatically preferable?

a) Spain is a country which I have always wanted to visit.

b) I have always wanted to visit Spain.

22.31. Consider the words *less* and *fewer* in these passages and identify the correctly written sentence.

a) He had *less* men than in the previous campaign

b) He had *fewer* men than in the previous campaign

22.32. Which sentence is most likely to escape criticism from the Grammar Police?

a) In connection with the anticipated visit of Prince Khalid to America, it is interesting to recall that he was once poor.

b) Interestingly, Prince Khalid, who is expected to soon visit America, was once poor.

c) Prince Khalid, who it is expected will soon visit America, was once poor.

d) All of these passages are written correctly.

22.33. Use *fact* only for matters that can directly verified, not matters of judgment. That a certain event happened on a given date is a fact; but such conclusions as that the climate of California is delightful or that the cost of living is sky-high these days, however incontestable they may be, are not properly facts.

a) True

b) False

22.34. Consider the use of *rather* and *kind of* in these constructions and choose the correctly written sentence.

a) David was *rather* disappointed when his girlfriend told him that she had to work Saturday night.

b) David was *kind of* disappointed when his girlfriend told him that she had to work Saturday night.

22.35. *Line* used in the sense of *course of procedure, conduct, thought,* is allowable, but has been so much overworked, especially in the phrase *along these lines*, that it should be discarded entirely.

a) True

b) False

22.36. "Jacob's troubles are less than mine" means that Jacob's troubles are not so great as mine.

a) True

b) False

22.37. Consider the use of *rather, kind of,* and *sort of* in these sentences and choose the grammatically correct form.

a) Amber is sort of a fossil resin.

b) Amber is a kind of fossil resin.

c) Amber is rather like a fossil resin.

22.38. *Less* refers to number, and *fewer* refers to quantity.

a) True

b) False

22.39. The word *like* is often misused for *as.* Which sentence is written correctly?

a) We spent the evening *like* in the old days.

b) We spent the evening *as* in the old days.

c) We spent the evening *as like* we did in the old days.

d) None of these sentences are correct.

22.40. The word *as* governs nouns and pronouns. Before phrases and clauses, the equivalent word is *like.*

a) True

b) False

22.41. Which form is grammatically correct?

a) Mr. B. also spoke along the same lines.

b) Mr. B. also spoke, to the same effect.

22.42. Which sentence is written correctly?

a) He is studying French literature.

b) He is studying along the line of French literature.

22.43. Which phrase is written correctly?

a) a literal flood of abuse

b) a flood of abuse

22.44. Consider the use of *like* and *as* in these sentences and choose the grammatically correct construction.

a) He thought *as* I did.

b) He thought *like* I did.

22.45. Which phrase is written correctly?

a) literally dead with fatigue

b) almost dead with fatigue

22.46. *Most* and *almost* are synonymous and can be used interchangeably.

a) True

b) False

22.47. Consider the use of *most* and *almost* in these sentences and choose the grammatically correct form.

a) *Almost* everybody at the party had too much to drink.

b) *Most* everybody at the party had too much to drink.

22.48. Which sentence is written correctly?

a) Joshua was optimistic *most all the time.*

b) Joshua was optimistic *most nearly all the time.*

c) Joshua was optimistic *almost all the time.*

22.49. Which sentence is written correctly?

a) The army engaged in acts of a hostile nature.

b) The army engaged in hostile acts.

c) The army engaged in literally hostile acts.

d) None of these sentences are correct.

22.50. You should avoid beginning paragraphs with *one of the most*, as, "One of the most interesting developments of modern science…" There is nothing wrong with this construction, Prof. Strunk advises; it is simply overused and threadbare.

a) True

b) False

22.51. Choose the grammatically preferable construction.

a) Switzerland is *one of the most* beautiful countries of Europe.

b) Switzerland is *among the most* beautiful countries of Europe.

22.52. Consider the use of the singular *has* and plural *have* in these phrases and select the correctly written sentence.

a) One of the ablest men that *has* attacked this problem

b) One of the ablest men that *have* attacked this problem

22.53. Strunk's rule of thumb is that any clumsily worded sentence should be recast. Similarly, if the use of the possessive is awkward or impossible, the sentence should be recast. With these rules in mind, which phrase should be rewritten?

a) In the event of a reconsideration of the whole matter's becoming necessary

b) If it should become necessary to reconsider the whole matter

22.54. Usually, the words *respective* and *respectively* can be omitted from a sentence without altering its meaning.

a) True

b) False

22.55. Identify the grammatically flawed sentence in need of rewriting.

a) There was great dismay that the judge should have decided in favor of the company.

b) There was great dismay that the judge ruled against the company.

c) There was great dismay with the decision of the judge being favorable to the company.

22.56. *Possess* should not be used as a mere substitute for *have* or *own*.

a) True

b) False

22.57. *The people* is a political term, not to be confused with *the public*. From the people comes political support or opposition; from the public comes artistic appreciation or commercial patronage.

a) True

b) False

22.58. Which construction is grammatically preferable?

a) He possessed great courage.

b) He had great courage.

22.59. Which form is preferable?

a) He was the fortunate possessor of

b) He owned

22.60. Which construction should you avoid in writing?

a) popular with the student body

b) popular with the students

22.61. Which form is preferable?

a) Works of fiction are listed under the names of their respective authors.

b) Works of fiction are listed under the names of their authors.

22.62. Which of these sentences reflect better grammar?

a) The one-mile and two-mile runs were won by Jones and by Cummings.

b) The one-mile and two-mile runs were won by Jones and Cummings respectively.

22.63. For the following conditional statement in first person, which form is correct?

a) I would not have succeeded without his help.

b) I should not have succeeded without his help.

c) I won't have succeeded without his help.

22.64. It is good practice to use *state* as a substitute for *say* or *remark*.

a) True

b) False

22.65. If we adhere to Strunk's rules on the proper use of *state* and *say* or *remark*, only one of these sentences is written correctly. Identify that sentence.

a) You should state whether you prefer vanilla or strawberry ice cream.

b) You should remark whether you prefer vanilla or strawberry ice cream.

c) He refused to say his objections.

d) He refused to state his objections.

22.66. It is better to use *student body* than *students* because it sounds more official.

a) True

b) False

22.67. As a general rule, writers should use *while* only with strict literalness, in the sense of *during the time that*.

a) True

b) False

22.68. Which construction reflects better grammar?

a) The students passed the budget resolution.

b) The student body passed the budget resolution.

22.69. *Shall* is widely used today in technical and academic writing.

a) True

b) False

22.70. Which sentence should be rewritten?

a) The office and salesrooms are on the ground floor; the rest of the building is devoted to manufacturing.

b) The office and salesrooms are on the ground floor, while the rest of the building is devoted to manufacturing.

22.71. The word *very* should be used sparingly because it is overused and other strong words can be substituted for better effect.

a) True

b) False

22.72. You should avoid the indiscriminate use of *while* in place of *and*, *but*, and *although*.

a) True

b) False

22.73. Strunk advises that the phrase *thanking you in advance* should be avoided in correspondence because:

a) There's no guarantee that you'll be happy with the person's response.

b) It's an old-fashioned phrase and should be replaced with something more upbeat and modern.

c) It sounds as if the writer meant, "It will not be worth my while to write to you again."

d) Thanking someone in advance is a sign of weakness.

22.74. Many writers use *while* as a substitute for *and* or *but;* in such uses, however, it is best replaced by a semicolon.

a) True

b) False

22.75. Which sentence is written correctly?

a) While the temperature may reach 95 degrees Fahrenheit in the daytime, the nights are often chilly.

b) Although the temperature may reach 95 degrees Fahrenheit in the daytime, the nights are often chilly.

22.76. The word *worthwhile* is overworked as a term of vague approval (and when used with *not,* of disapproval). It should only be used with nouns, as, "That sci-fi novel is a worthwhile book."

a) True

b) False

22.77. Which form is written correctly?

a) His books are not worthwhile.

b) His books are not worth reading.

c) Both sentences are written correctly.

d) Neither sentence is written correctly.

22.78. The use of *worthwhile* before a noun, as in "a worthwhile story," is bad grammar and should be avoided.

a) True

b) False

Quiz #23
Misused Words & Expressions (Part 2)

This quiz module applies only to Strunk's first edition of *The Elements of Style* and the 2018 Classic Edition. Readers of the Strunk & White edition should skip to Quiz #24.

Some questions on this quiz contain italicized text directing your attention to words or expressions you should evaluate. Consider the italicized words to determine the correct answer for each question.

23.01. Some writers resort to using *lose out* as a more emphatic expression than *lose*, but it is actually less so because of its commonness.

a) True

b) False

23.02. If you follow Prof. Strunk's advice on using the word *dependable*, which construction is the better choice?

a) Martha is a *dependable* friend who always has a bright smile or a kind word.

b) Martha is a *reliable* friend who always has a bright smile or a kind word.

23.03. Which construction does a better job of avoiding word clutter?

a) Dayton has adopted the commission system of government.

b) Dayton has adopted government by commission.

c) The city of Dayton has officially adopted the system of government by commission.

23.04. Considering Strunk's advice on using the word *dependable*, which construction is the better choice?

a) I am quite certain Jose is trustworthy and would never steal from the cash drawer.

b) I am quite certain Jose is dependable and would never steal from the cash drawer.

23.05. *Don't* is a contraction that can be written in place of either *do not* or *does not*.

a) True

b) False

23.06. In American English, *fix* should only be used in technical and other formal writing when you mean:

a) arrange, prepare, mend

b) fasten, make firm or immovable, etc.

c) Both a and b are correct.

d) *Fix* should not be used in formal writing.

23.07. Which sentence is written correctly?

a) The Gonzales family lives in the near by community.

b) The Gonzales family lives in the neighboring community.

23.08. According to Prof. Strunk, *ofttimes* and *oftentimes* are archaic forms, and *often* should be substituted instead.

a) True

b) False

23.09. It is acceptable and sometimes preferable to use "so" as an intensifier; for example, *so good, so warm*.

a) True

b) False

23.10. When you need to write out a number, which form is grammatically preferable:

a) one hundred twenty hours

b) one-hundred-twenty hours

c) one hundred and twenty hours

d) a, b and c are correct

e) None of these answers are correct.

23.11. Which construction effectively avoids word clutter?

a) The army relies on the dormitory system to house troops during boot camp training.

b) The army relies on dormitories to house troops during boot camp training.

23.12. When it comes to writing about a candidate expressing an opinion, which sentence contains faulty grammar?

a) The candidate did not hesitate to express his point of view on immigration.

b) The candidate did not hesitate to express his viewpoint on immigration.

c) The candidate did not hesitate to express his opinion on immigration.

23.13. Which sentence is written correctly?

a) His brother, *whom* he said would send him the money, mysteriously disappeared.

b) His brother, *who* he said would send him the money, mysteriously disappeared.

23.14. Which construction is grammatically correct?

a) The man *whom* he thought was his friend

b) The man *who* he thought was his friend

23.15. Which construction is grammatically correct?

a) The man *who* he thought was his friend

b) The man *whom* he thought his friend

c) Both sentences are written correctly.

d) Both sentences are written incorrectly.

Quiz #24
Misused Words & Expressions
(Part 3)

This quiz module is for readers of Strunk & White's *Elements of Style*. Readers of Strunk's first edition and the 2018 Classic Edition can self-test on commonly misused words and expressions with Quiz #22 and #23. As with the preceding module, some questions on this quiz contain italicized text directing your attention to words or expressions to evaluate. Consider the italicized words to determine the correct answer for each question.

24.01. The words *irritate* and *aggravate* mean the same and may be used interchangeably.

a) True

b) False

24.02. Which sentence uses the italicized word correctly?

a) The lonely old woman often *alluded* to the fact that her son never had time to visit her.

b) The lonely old woman often *eluded* to the fact that her son never had time to visit her.

c) Both a and b are written correctly.

24.03. Which sentence uses the italicized word correctly?

a) The new blood pressure medication is more expensive, and it *irritates* her vertigo.

b) The new blood pressure medication is more expensive, and it *aggravates* her vertigo.

24.04. Which sentence uses the italicized word correctly?

a) That scratchy fabric *irritates* Julia's skin.

b) That scratchy fabric *aggravates* Julia's skin.

24.06. Which sentence is written correctly?

a) The burglar *eluded* police by fleeing into a dark alley.

b) The burglar *alluded* police by fleeing into a dark alley.

24.05. Which sentence uses the italicized word correctly?

a) The child's crying is *aggravating* to him.

b) The child's crying is *irritating* to him.

24.07. Which sentence is written correctly?

a) No matter how many books the writer has published, success still *eludes* him.

b) No matter how many books the writer has published, success still *alludes* him.

24.08. Which sentence uses the italicized word correctly?

a) The voters saw through the scheme and realized that the tax cut was an *elusion*; they would owe more at tax time.

b) The voters saw through the scheme and realized that the tax cut was an *allusion*; they would owe more at tax time.

c) The voters saw through the scheme and realized that the tax cut was an *illusion*; they would owe more at tax time.

24.09. Which sentence uses the italicized word correctly?

a) The judge announced that Carolyn had been selected as an *alternative* juror.

b) The judge announced that Carolyn had been selected as an *alternate* juror.

24.10. Which sentence is written correctly?

a) The senator made an *illusion* to the tax benefits included in the proposed legislation.

b) The senator made an *elusion* to the tax benefits included in the proposed legislation.

c) The senator made an *allusion* to the tax benefits included in the proposed legislation.

24.11. Which sentence is written correctly?

a) The bank robber's *allusion* of detectives enabled him to rob yet another bank in Iowa.

b) The bank robber's *elusion* of detectives enabled him to rob yet another bank in Iowa.

c) The bank robber's *illusion* of detectives enabled him to rob yet another bank in Iowa.

24.12. Which passage uses both italicized words correctly?

a) The doctor made several *allusions* to a diet plan and warned the obese patient that he should have no *illusions* about over-the-counter medications being of much benefit.

b) The doctor made several *elusions* to a diet plan and warned the obese patient that he should have no *allusions* about over-the-counter medications being of much benefit.

c) The doctor made several *illusions* to a diet plan and warned the obese patient that he should have no *allusions* about over-the-counter medications being of much benefit.

24.13. Which sentence uses the italicized word correctly?

a) No *alternate* energy source is as cheap as natural gas.

b) No *alternative* energy source is as cheap as natural gas.

24.14. Which sentence uses the italicized word correctly?

a) The student dropped out of college, announcing that she wanted to pursue an *alternative* lifestyle.

b) The student dropped out of college, announcing that she wanted to pursue an *alternate* lifestyle.

24.15. The words *anticipate* and *expect* have the same meaning and can be used interchangeably.

a) True

b) False

24.16. Which of these sentences is written correctly?

a) It was rumored that Megan was homesick and wanted to be back in New York *between* friends.

b) It was rumored that Megan was homesick and wanted to be back in New York *among* friends.

24.17. Which sentence is grammatically correct?

a) I gave Jessica and Pierre some cake and told them to share it *between* them.

b) I gave Jessica and Pierre some cake and told them to share it *among* them.

24.18. Which secluded campsite is described correctly?

a) The secluded campsite is hidden *among* the pine trees.

b) The secluded campsite is hidden *between* the pine trees.

24.19. Which statement is grammatically correct?

a) I don't taste a difference *among* the red apples and the yellow ones.

b) I don't taste a difference *between* the red apples and the yellow ones.

24.20. Which sentence uses the italicized word correctly?

a) The Google Maps app directed me to take an *alternate* route to reach my destination.

b) The Google Maps app directed me to take an *alternative* route to reach my destination.

24.21. The difference between *anybody* and *anyone* is subtle but distinct. The former means "any human" and can encompass a group of people; the latter means "any one person."

a) True

b) False

24.22. Which construction is grammatically preferable?

a) You must *contact* your math professor to discuss your exam grade.

b) You must *get in touch* with your math professor to discuss your exam grade.

24.23. The expression *as yet* should only be used at the beginning of a sentence. For instance: *As yet (or so far), the wildflowers have not bloomed.*

a) True
b) False

24.24. Which sentence is written correctly?

a) Senator McAllen is widely regarded *as being* the most conservative member on the committee.
b) Senator McAllen is widely regarded *as* the most conservative member on the committee.

24.25. The expression *and/or* is a lazy short-cut that often creates ambiguity and should be avoided in writing.

a) True
b) False

24.26. Which sentence is written correctly?

a) The local election results have not been announced *as yet.*
b) The local election results have not been announced *yet.*
c) The local election results weren't *yet* announced.

24.27. Which sentence is written correctly?

a) Magdalena *could care less* about her parents' opinion.
b) Magdalena *could not care less* about her parents' opinion.

24.28. The problem with the phrase *I could care less* is that it is missing the word *not* and thus implies that you do care, and thus it is possible for you to care less.

a) True
b) False

24.29. The word *comprise* means "to contain" or "to be made up of." For example, "The house comprises five rooms" means it contains five rooms.

a) True
b) False

24.30. The expression *currently* is usually redundant and should be written out of every sentence.

a) True
b) False

24.31. Which one of the following sentences avoids redundancy?

a) The company is currently accepting applications for the position of senior engineer.
b) Currently, the company is accepting applications for the position of senior engineer.
c) The software company is accepting applications for the position of senior engineer.

24.32. Which sentence uses *disinterested* correctly?

a) He was so *disinterested* in the trial that he fell asleep while the prosecutor was questioning the witness.
b) The plaintiff is obviously *disinterested* in the excuses put forward by the defendant.
c) The court-appointed mediator should be a *disinterested* party in the dispute.

24.33. If you are *disinterested*, it means you are _____.

a) not interested
b) apathetic
c) unable to comprehend what is going on
d) impartial

24.34. The expression *each and every one* should be avoided in most forms of writing.

a) True
b) False

24.35. The word *infer* means hinting at something, and *imply* means making an educated guess.

a) True
b) False

24.36. Which sentence contains a grammar error that writers should avoid?

a) Each and every one of those men worked hard for their wages.

b) Every one of those men worked hard for their wages.

c) Each of those men worked hard for their wages.

24.37. Which sentence conveys Jose's enthusiasm using proper grammar?

a) Jose was enthused about receiving his law degree.

b) Jose enthused about receiving his law degree.

c) Jose was enthusiastic about receiving his law degree.

24.38. Which sentence is written correctly?

a) The newspaper should publish its expose of corruption in our city, *regardless* of the fallout that might occur.

b) The newspaper should publish its expose of corruption in our city, *irregardless* of the fallout that might occur.

c) Both sentences are written correctly.

24.39. Which sentence offers the most clarity on the event being described.

a) The convict escaped and fled into the woods.

b) The convict escaped from the courthouse and fled into the woods.

c) The convict escaped from the facility and fled into the woods.

24.40. Which form uses *further* correctly?

a) The astronomer delved *further* into the mysterious signal from deep space.

b) The two men jogged for one hour, but the older man ran *further* than the younger man did.

c) Both sentences use *further* correctly.

24.41. Which sentence uses the word *farther* correctly?

a) The astronomer delved *farther* into the mysterious signal from deep space.

b) The two men jogged for one hour, but the older man ran *farther* than the younger man

24.42. In most instances, the term *facility* should be replaced with a more descriptive noun; for example, write "court" or "schoolhouse" instead.

a) True

b) False

24.43. Which construction uses the word *gratuitous* incorrectly?

a) Joseph's harsh words seemed *gratuitous*.

b) That risqué scene in the movie was *gratuitous* and should have been cut out.

c) The punishment seemed harsh and *gratuitous*.

d) None of these sentences are incorrect.

24.44. Which sentence uses the italicized word correctly?

a) The stock broker *implied* that his client's entire investment might be at risk.

b) The defense lawyer *inferred* to the judge that his client was guilty.

c) Both sentences are written correctly.

24.45. Which sentence uses the italicized word correctly?

a) His tone of voice and guilty expression *inferred* that he was lying about where he was on the night in question.

b) I didn't mean to *infer* that you were wrong.

c) Neither sentence is written correctly.

24.46. Which sentence uses the italicized word correctly?

a) Am I right to *infer* that you think I am a lousy writer?

b) Carla's drama coach *inferred* that she did not have much talent and should not quit her day job.

24.49. You should use the expression *inside of* only in the adverbial sense of "in less than," as, "I will be home inside of an hour." Otherwise, you should omit "of" and simply write "inside."

a) True

b) False

24.47. Which sentence is grammatically correct?

a) Importantly, your lottery prize will be paid in cash.

b) Most importantly, your lottery prize will be paid in cash.

c) Most important, your lottery prize will be paid in cash.

d) None of these sentences are correct.

24.48. The word *nauseated* means "causing nausea," and *nauseous* means "feeling sick."

a) True

b) False

24.50. Which sentence reflects the best grammatical style?

a) *Inside of* the box, the clerk placed five cans of cleanser.

b) *Inside* the box, the clerk placed five cans of cleanser.

c) Both sentences are written correctly.

24.51. The word *insightful* is often used as an exaggeration for "perceptive" and should only be used to denote a high degree of perception that would qualify as genuine insight.

a) True

b) False

24.52. Which sentence is grammatically incorrect?

a) *In regard to* your question, I'll do some research and get back to you with an answer.

b) *In regards to* your question, I'll do some research and get back to you with an answer.

c) *As regards your question*, I'll do some research and get back to you with an answer.

24.53. Adding the *-ir* prefix to *regardless* forms a nonsensical expression, *irregardless*, which should never be used in writing.

a) True

b) False

24.54. Writers often confuse *lay* and *lie*, but it is easy to remember the difference in present tense: *lay* requires an object, such as you lay a book on the desk, and lie doesn't (so you lie on the grass and watch the clouds).

a) True

b) False

24.55. Which construction uses the present tense of *lie* correctly?

a) I lay down on the floor to stretch my back.

b) I laid down on the floor to stretch my back.

c) I lie down on the floor to stretch my back.

24.56. Which construction uses the past tense of *lie* correctly?

a) Yesterday, I lay there remembering our trip to Hawaii.

b) Yesterday, I laid there remembering our trip to Hawaii.

c) Yesterday, I lied there remembering our trip to Hawaii.

24.57. Which construction uses the past participle of *lie* correctly?

a) But I forgot that I had laid there the day before enjoying the same fond memory.

b) But I forgot that I had lain there the day before enjoying the same fond memory.

c) But I forgot that I had lied there the day before enjoying the same fond memory.

24.58. Which construction uses the present tense of *lay* correctly?

a) As I walk by, I lay the book on the desk.

b) As I walk by, I laid the book on the desk.

c) As I walk by, I lie the book on the desk.

24.59. Which sentence uses the past tense of *lay* correctly?

a) As I walked by, I lain the book on the desk.

b) As I walked by, I lie the book on the desk.

c) As I walked by, I laid the book on the desk.

24.60. Which construction uses the past participle of *lay* correctly?

a) I had laid the book on the desk.

b) I had lain the book on the desk.

c) I had lied the book on the desk.

24.61. Some writers confuse *leave,* which means to depart from a place, and *let,* which means to directly or inadvertently allow something to happen.

a) True

b) False

24.62. Which form is written incorrectly?

a) *Leave* my office immediately!

b) *Let* me think about it for a few minutes.

c) I thought about it, and I'm willing to *leave* it go.

d) At what time does your flight leave for Ohio?

24.63. As an adjective, *meaningful* is vague and threadbare. You should replace it with another more relevant or specific adjective.

a) True

b) False

24.64. Which construction is grammatically unsound?

a) Laura changed Bob's life in many ways.

b) Laura changed Bob's life in ways that made him a better person.

c) Laura changed Bob's life in meaningful ways.

24.65. Which sentence is written correctly?

a) *The fact is,* Trevon lives in poverty, yet he is the smartest teenager in the class.

b) When you believe in yourself, *the fact is,* you can go far in life.

c) *The fact is* clear to all who read Ed's book.

24.66. *Nauseousness* is a medical condition that arises from a feeling of being nauseous.

a) True

b) False

24.67. *Nor* and *or* are often confused and used incorrectly in writing. Which sentence is written correctly?

a) I don't like beer nor wine nor vodka.

b) I like neither beer or wine or vodka.

c) I don't like either beer nor wine or vodka.

d) None of the answers are written correctly.

24.68. *Ongoing* is often redundant and adds nothing to a sentence; occasionally, however, its use is appropriate. Choose the sentence in which *ongoing* is used correctly.

a) Paul enjoyed participating in the *ongoing* band practice.

b) Loud music blaring in the college dorm posed an *ongoing* problem.

c) The fundraising campaign for the domestic violence shelter is *ongoing.*

24.69. *Personally* is often a threadbare adverb that adds nothing to a sentence; or it is used incorrectly as a substitute for "personal." Which sentence uses *personally* correctly?

a) I was *personally* involved with the decision to hire Bob.

b) *Personally,* I believe he was the most qualified candidate.

c) Address any complaints about Bob to me *personally.*

e) None of the sentences are use *personally* correctly.

24.70. *Presently* can mean "at the present time" or "soon; in a short time." E. B. White advises that substituting the word for *currently* may lead to confusion, and *presently* should be limited to the latter meaning. If you follow that advice, which sentence uses *presently* correctly?

a) He is *presently* standing outdoors in the sleet and rain.

b) The train from Chicago will be arriving *presently.*

c) *Presently,* Elizabeth is away from her desk.

24.71. If you are *nauseated*, you are about to throw up. If you are *nauseous*, you are offensive and about to make someone else to throw up.

a) True

b) False

24.72. Which sentence is written correctly?

a) My son's behavior was *regretful*; but I assure you it will not happen again.

b) I feel *regrettable* that I borrowed your phone and lost it.

c) The cruise ship sank in the harbor as it embarked on its maiden voyage, which was a *regrettable* start.

24.73. Which sentence uses *that* or *which* incorrectly?

a) You must continually seek knowledge in a world *which* is constantly changing.

b) The medicine *that* he takes for high blood pressure is on the kitchen counter.

c) Pies *that* contain fruit fillings are my favorite dessert.

24.74. Which construction uses *that* or *which* incorrectly?

a) You must continually seek knowledge in a world *that* is constantly changing.

b) The medicine *that* he takes for high blood pressure is on the kitchen counter.

c) Pies *which* contain fruit fillings are my favorite dessert.

24.75. Which sentence is written correctly?

a) *The truth is*, I've been having headaches for days with no relief.

b) *The truth is* stranger than fiction.

c) I moved from Nevada to New Mexico, and *the truth is*, I'll move back as soon as I can.

24.76. *The foreseeable future* is a hackneyed and ambiguous expression that should be avoided in formal writing.

a) True

b) False

24.77. Which form is written incorrectly?

a) The young soldier did not expect to be captured by rebel troops and forced to endure a *torturous* ordeal.

b) The legislation went through a *tortuous* process before the bill passed the Senate.

c) The limo driver took a *torturous* route through the city.

24.78. *Torturous* means "full of twists and turns," and *tortuous* means "involving or causing torture."

a) True

b) False

24.79. Which sentence uses *thrust* in a way that would make any grammar purist groan?

a) He *thrust* his hands into his pockets and gasped when he realized that the fifty-dollar bill he'd slipped into his pocket an hour ago was missing.

b) Mr. Miller's campaign for a seat in the state senate has tremendous *thrust*.

c) *Thrust* is the force that moves a rocket off the ground and into space.

24.80. Which sentence is written correctly?

a) The path to peace in the Middle East has been *torturous* from the beginning.

b) Miraculously, he survived the *tortuous* interrogation with only cuts and bruises, a black eye, and a broken arm.

c) The police nabbed the bank robber after a *tortuous* chase through the underground labyrinth of sewer canals.

24.81. Which phrase is grammatically correct?

a) The painting was *very unique*.

b) The painting was the *most unique*.

c) That painting was *more unique* than his first work.

d) All three sentences are written correctly.

e) None of these sentences are written correctly—if something is unique, it's one of a kind, with no comparison.

24.82. It is acceptable to write either *try and* or *try to* ("try and start the car," "try to start the car"); but the latter is more precise and should be used in formal writing.

a) True

b) False

24.83. Which sentence is grammatically preferable?

a) You must *try to repair* the broken window in the kitchen before the storm arrives on Friday.

b) You must *try and repair* the broken window in the kitchen before the storm arrives on Friday.

24.84. The word *unique* has a superlative form, so it is proper to write that something is unique, very unique, more unique, or the most unique.

a) True

b) False

24.85. The words *use* and *utilize* mean the same and may be used interchangeably in your writing.

a) True

b) False

24.86. To *utilize* something means to employ it for a certain purpose; to *use* something means to employ it in a creative, unexpected, or exemplary way.

a) True

b) False

24.87. Which sentence is written correctly?

a) Do you have a pencil I can *use*?

b) Do you have a pencil I can *utilize*?

24.88. Which sentence is written correctly?

a) I can *utilize* my hairbrush to remove snow from the windshield.

b) I can *use* my hairbrush to remove snow from the windshield?

24.89. Which form is written correctly?

a) Although it was the busiest time of the year for retail, Mr. Jones promised his family that he would *try and take off* the weekend.

b) Although it was the busiest time of the year for retail, Mr. Jones promised his family that he would *try to take off* the weekend.

23.90. Which sentence is written correctly?

a) What kind of shovel can I *utilize* to remove the snow?

b) What kind of shovel can I *use* to remove the snow?

24.91. Which sentence uses the italicized word correctly?

a) Maryanne *utilized* the flashlight to illuminate the garage.

b) Maryanne *used* the flashlight to illuminate the garage.

c) Both sentences are written correctly.

24.92. Some writers tack the suffix *-wise* onto a plethora of nouns, but most such constructions are ill-advised. One of the few exceptions to this rule is in the word *clockwise*.

a) True

b) False

Section 5
Commonly Misspelled Words

Quiz #25
Commonly Misspelled Words (Part 1)

As Strunk explains: "The spelling of English words is not fixed and invariable, nor does it depend on any other authority than general agreement. In this day and age, agreement as to the spelling of most words is practically unanimous. At any given moment, however, a relatively small number of words may be spelled in more than one way. As one of these forms comes to be generally preferred, the less customary form comes to look obsolete and is discarded. From time to time new forms, mostly simplifications, are introduced by innovators, and either win their place or die of neglect."

Hundreds of commonly misspelled words cause headaches for writers and students. Strunk included a list of 65 such words in Chapter IV of his book, which was omitted from E.B. White's fourth edition but returned in the 2018 Classic Edition, which encompasses nearly 200 problematic words. Both lists are included in this workbook: the words from Strunk's first edition are covered in Quiz #25, and the extended list from the 2018 Classic Edition is given in Quiz #26.

To test yourself on commonly misspelled words in Strunk's first edition and the 2018 Classic Edition, complete these sentences with the correctly spelled word.

25.01. The taxi driver _____ veered off the winding country road and into the ditch.
a) accidently
b) accidentally
c) accidentaly
d) accidentilly

25.02. The historic role of the United States Senate is to _____ and consent.
a) advise
b) advize
c) advice

25.03. Mr. Lopez, the guidance counselor at our college, always gives good _____.
a) advise
b) advize
c) advice

25.04. The jet suddenly made a U-turn and changed _____.
a) coarce
b) course
c) coarse

25.05. The gloomy weather in Seattle may tend to _____ your mood.
a) affect
c) effect

25.06. The fraudster was able to _____ his victims.
a) deceive
b) deceive
c) deseive
d) deseeve

25.07. _____ must evacuate the building at once!
a) Everyone
b) Every one

25.08. The detective surmised that _____ of those men might be the thief.
a) anyone
b) any one

25.09. _____ who ventures into that remote wilderness risks being killed by hostile natives or wild beasts.
a) Anyone
b) Any one

25.10. When I go to the grocery store, it is hard to _____ food costs so much.
a) I
b) beleave
c) believe

25.11. The wealthy industrialist's substantial donations _____ a worthy cause.

a) benafit

b) benefit

c) benifit

25.12. The protesters accomplished their goal at the rally, which was to _____ the status quo.

a) challenge

b) challendge

c) challienge

25.13. That grade of sandpaper is very _____.

a) course

b) cource

c) coarse

25.14. That supervisor is not well liked because he will often _____ his workers.

a) criticise

b) critisize

c) criticize

25.15. It might be hard to fathom, but there is a _____ moral to this story.

a) definite

b) defenite

c) definite

d) defanite

25.16. The detective asked, "Can you _____ the man who robbed the bank?"

a) describe

b) discribe

c) desscribe

25.17. Some people fear the unknown and _____ what they do not understand.

a) dispise

b) despise

c) despize

d) dispize

25.18. According to the weather forecast, a major snowstorm is expected to _____ over the Rockies tonight.

a) develope

b) develop

c) develupe

25.19. You will surely _____ yourself if you wear that dress out in public.

a) embarress

b) embarrass

c) embarass

25.20. The young girl tried very hard not to _____ her parents.

a) disappoint

b) dissapoint

c) dissipoint

25.21. An hour after dawn, the dense fog began to _____.

a) dissipitate

b) disapate

c) dissipate

25.22. That small bolt serves a ____ purpose.

a) dual

b) dewl

c) duel

25.23. A feeling of _____ came over the climber when he reached the top of the mountain.

a) estasy

b) ecstasy

c) ecstacey

25.24. The acclaimed physicist affirmed his belief in the _____ of extraterrestrial life.

a) existance

b) existense

c) existence

d) existince

25.25. The tranquilizer had no _____ on the raging bull.

a) effect
b) affect

25.26. It might surprise you, but I have read _____ of Stephen King's books.

a) everyone
b) every one

25.27. Tragically, _____ of the turtles that washed up on the shore was frozen.

a) everyone
b) every one

25.28. That man has the power to _____ every woman he meets.

a) fasinate
b) facsinate
c) fascinate

25.29. The four-story office building was destroyed by a _____ explosion.

a) feiry
b) fiery
c) firey

25.30. That police detective was _____ a Navy seal.

a) formerly
b) formarly
c) formally

25.31. To be honest, Ted's joke was not _____ and no one laughed.

a) humorous
b) humorus
c) humerous

25.32. The politician's _____ was on full display when he contradicted what he had said last week and denied his prior claim.

a) hippocrisy
b) hypocricey
c) hypocrisy

25.33. When a ghostly hand hurled a glass vase across the room and it shattered against the fireplace mantle, the terrified girl _____ ran outdoors.

a) immedeately
b) immediately
c) immedietly

25.34. That man is not a police officer—he's an _____!

a) imposter
b) impostor
c) impostore

25.35. The bizarre _____ made Tyrone and his friends fear for their lives.

a) incident
b) insident
c) insedent

25.36. That scientific theory was discussed at the seminar, but only _____.

a) insidentally
b) incidently
c) incidentally

25.37. Vitamins C and D are both essential, but you should note that the _____ is a hormone, not a vitamin.

a) latter
b) later

25.38. If you _____ your keys, you will be locked out of your house and will need to call a locksmith.

a) loose
b) lose

25.39. William and Lucy reaffirmed their _____ vows at a romantic getaway in Hawaii.

a) marriege
b) marriage
c) marriadge
d) mairrage

25.40. The children always seem to get into _____ when they are left alone for more than a few minutes.

a) mischief

b) mischeif

c) mischefe

25.41. Dr. Fung diagnosed the patient with indigestion and a heart _____.

a) murmer

b) murmur

c) murmurr

25.42. Like it or not, it's a fact that money is a _____ evil in today's world.

a) necessary

b) necessarie

c) necassary

25.43. The tragic accident on the bridge _____ early last month.

a) occured

b) occurred

c) ocurred

25.44. If you want _____ to come knocking, you must be ready and willing to answer the door.

a) oppertunity

b) opportunity

c) opportunite

25.45. Did Einstein believe that humans exist here on earth and at the same time coexist in a _____ universe?

a) parallel

b) paralel

c) parallel

25.46. Neil Simon was a prolific _____.

a) playwrite

b) playwright

c) playright

25.47. In the weeks _____ the election, pollsters made wildly differing predictions about the outcome.

a) preceeding

b) preseading

c) preceding

25.48. The man's vile remarks revealed the depth of his _____ and hatred of his neighbors.

a) predjudice

b) prejudise

c) prejudice

25.49. Ms. Chang, the high school _____, expelled both students for vaping in the bathroom.

a) principal

b) principle

d) princapal

25.50. Though controversial, that scientific _____ is based on solid evidence.

a) principal

b) principle

c) princapel

25.51. In America, voting is a right, and driving a car is a _____.

a) privilege

b) priviledge

c) privaledge

25.52. The woman seemed quite happy as she read her child's favorite nursery _____.

a) rhime

b) rhymme

c) rhyme

25.53. Vanessa might _____ a degree in law.

a) persue

b) pursue

c) pursew

25.54. Making the same point three times in an essay is unnecessary _____.

a) repatition

b) repitition

c) repetition

25.55. Uncle Bill had no sense of _____ whatsoever and made a fool of himself on the dance floor.

a) rhythum

b) rhythm

c) rhythem

25.56. That is a ____ excuse for missing work!

a) ridiculus

b) ridiculous

c) rediculous

25.57. Many church leaders condemned the book as _____.

a) sacriligeous

b) sacralegeous

c) sacrilegious

25.58. The barbarian invaders attempted to _____ the palace but were repelled by the king's brave fighters.

a) seaize

b) seize

c) sieze

25.59. The two strangers met, exchanged a few words, and then went their _____ ways.

a) separate

b) seperate

c) seperite

25.60. As the weather turned cold, the _____ collected his flock and brought them down from the hills.

a) shephard

b) shepherd

c) sheperd

25.61. The Roman army laid _____ to the castle, and then they waited patiently for everyone inside to starve.

a) siege

b) seige

c) seage

25.62. Those two women look _____ in a number of ways, but it is obvious they are not related.

a) simmilar

b) simaler

c) similar

d) similer

25.63. A form of metaphor, a _____ is a figure of speech that compares one thing to another.

a) simale

b) simile

d) simalee

25.64. _____ has passed since we met for coffee at the local cafe.

a) Some time

b) Sometime

25.65. I will spend _____ in Dublin when I visit Ireland.

a) some time

b) sometime

25.66. We will go on a vacation together _____ soon.

a) some time

b) sometime

25.67. You can plainly see that the computer is not on my desk, so _____ must have taken it.

a) someone

b) some one

25.68. Roberto was just _____ smart for his own good.

a) to

b) two

c) too

25.69. He bought _____ coffees, but drank only one.

a) two

b) too

c) to

25.70. What happened to Megan was a _____, but she made the best of it.

a) tradgedy

b) tragedy

c) tragidy

25.71. Anya is _____ guilty of shoplifting because she was caught with two bottles of perfume in her purse.

a) undoubtibly

b) undoubtedly

c) undoubtadly

25.72. The protagonist of a story is the hero; the antagonist is the _____.

a) villain

b) villane

c) villain

Quiz #26
Commonly Misspelled Words (Part 2)

This quiz module is for readers of the 2018 Classic Edition, which includes a larger set of commonly misspelled words than Strunk's first edition offers. To self-test on this expanded word list, complete the following sentences with the correctly spelled word.

26.01. You've no doubt heard the old adage that _____ makes the heart grow fonder.

a) absense

b) absince

c) absence

26.02. Professor Kirk gave the essay a C grade because the student's work was _____ but not exemplary.

a) acceptible

b) acceptable

c) aceptable

26.03. The chair was not sturdy enough to _____ the large man's weight, and it collapsed when he sat on it.

a) accomodate

b) accommodate

c) acommodate

26.04. The doctor wanted to _____ an understanding of the patient's symptoms before he prescribed medication.

a) aquire

b) acquire

c) acquier

26.05. If you want to elevate yourself from an _____ to a pro writer, you must first learn the fundamental rules of grammar.

a) amateur

b) amature

c) amatuer

26.06. The man began shouting and throwing food at frightened diners in the restaurant for no _____ reason.

a) apparant

b) apparent

c) apperant

26.07. Polar bears are struggling to survive, and many are dying of starvation, as temperatures rise in the _____ wilderness.

a) artic

b) arctec

c) arctic

d) archtec

26.08. It was a pointless _____ because the neighbors shouted threats and obscenities at one another, and nothing was settled.

a) arguement

b) argument

c) arguemint

26.09. One who does not believe in a supreme deity is referred to as an _____.

a) athiest

b) atheist

c) aetheist

26.10. Every life has a _____ and an end. If we are lucky, many years will transpire between the two, and at least some of those years will be happy ones.

a) begining

b) begininng

c) beginning

26.11. Samsung and Intel are the world's largest chipmakers, and they are the _____ for the PC market.

a) bellweather

b) bellwhether

c) bellwether

d) bellwither

26.12. Timothy burst into tears when he noticed that his _____ had been stolen, even though he had locked the chain.

a) bicicle

b) bicycle

c) bycycle

26.13. Former president George H. W. Bush intensely disliked _____ and once said that he never, ever, wanted to see another sprig of it on his plate

a) brocoli

b) broccoli

d) brocallie

26.14. Be sure to make a note of your appointment on the _____, or you might forget it.

a) calendar

b) calander

c) calender

26.15. The weather _____ predicted the approaching storm would bring sub-zero temperatures to the region.

a) bureau

b) beurow

c) burowe

26.16. Fernando sat at his desk, gazing up at the _____ and daydreaming rather than focusing on his math test, which was timed, and which he was almost certain to fail.

a) sealing

b) cealing

c) ceiling

26.17. Laura took flowers to the _____ and placed them on her father's grave to honor his memory.

a) cematery

b) cemetery

c) cemetary

26.18. Some states in the U.S. are suffering from extreme drought, but weather is _____, and the winter months could make the situation better or worse.

a) changable

b) changible

c) changeable

26.19. Every one of the athletes had a strong sense of _____ and mutual respect for her teammates.

a) camraderie

b) camaraderie

c) camaradorie

26.20. Every employer wants to hire _____ employees who are honest, dependable, and work hard.

a) conscientous

b) consientious

c) conscientious

26.21. The doctor informed us of our uncle's _____, and we all were stunned by the news.

a) deceise

b) decease

c) deseace

26.22. The saying, "Let your _____ be your guide is often thought to derive from the Bible; in fact, it is from Disney's story of *Pinocchio.*

a) conscence

b) conscience

c) conciance

26.23. The clinical trial reported that patients were grouped into more than one _____, depending on their symptoms and the degree of severity.

a) catagory

b) catagorie

c) category

26.24. What is lacking in our leaders today is a _____ of opinion on how to approach immigration reform.

a) consensis

b) consensus

c) consenssus

26.25. The investigative journalist sparked an uproar when he published a story in his newspaper _____, alleging that the pharmaceutical company knew its drug was unsafe and conspired to hide the truth.

a) column

b) colume

c) collume

26.26. Lisa's favorite drink is the strawberry _____, but she can never stop herself at just one.

a) daiquiri

b) daquirie

c) daquarie

26.27. Some believe that parents who fail to _____ their children do more harm than good; others disagree.

a) disipline

b) discipline

c) discipline

26.28. Driving up the mountain, we found that our car guzzled gasoline; but during our _____ down the other side, we coasted most of the way.

a) desent

b) descent

c) decent

26.29. Renters throughout California are in _____ need of affordable housing.

a) desparate

b) despirate

c) desperate

26.30. A bolt of lightning struck the tree with _____ consequences—less than thirty minutes later, a massive forest fire raged out of control.

a) disasterous

b) disastrouse

c) disastrous

26.31. The CEO _____ perjury because he lied on the witness stand under oath, and the prosecutor had evidence to prove it.

a) committed

b) comitted

c) commited

26.32. When the patrol car passed by and the policeman saw the man stumbling down the street, he was arrested for public _____.

a) drunkenness

b) drunkeness

c) drunkennese

26.33. Learning a _____ language can be a daunting task, though some languages are easier to learn than others.

a) forign

b) foreign

c) fourin

26.34. The farmer moved his tractor and other _____ into the barn the day before the first winter snow fell.

a) equipmint

b) equipment

c) eqwipment

26.35. If you want to be healthy and live to a ripe old age, it is imperative that you _____ for at least a half hour every day.

a) exercise

b) exersize

c) exercize

26.36. The blue sky, the sound of the waves, the sea breeze, and the vast ocean melting into the horizon will _____ you the first time, and perhaps every time, you see it.

a) exhilarate

b) exilarate

c) exhilerate

26.37. It is often said that _____ is the best teacher; but learning by trial and error is not the easiest way.

a) experiance

b) expirience

c) experience

26.38. Abraham Lincoln and George Washington both were born in the month of _____.

a) Februery

b) Febuary

c) February

26.39. LED light bulbs cost more to buy than fluorescent bulbs, but they are cheaper to operate and do not contain mercury, which can pose serious health hazards.

a) florescent

b) fluorescent

c) floresent

26.40. While exercising, your hands may become sweaty and you could lose your grip on the _____, possibly dropping it on your foot.

a) dumbell

b) dumbbell

c) dumbbelle

26.41. It is difficult to _____ a person's intentions from one conversation; but as the saying goes, actions speak louder than words.

a) gage

b) gaege

c) gauge

26.42. If you want to be at peace with life, a conscience and a well-defined moral compass are _____ .

a) indispensible
b) indespensable
c) indispensable

26.43. Many manufacturers offer a written _____ that their products will perform as intended for a certain amount of time.

a) garuntee
b) guarintee
c) guarantee

26.44. "The true sign of _____ is not knowledge but imagination." —Albert Einstein

a) intelligence
b) inteligence
c) intelligance

26.45. Abby was _____ for the opportunity to move away from the Midwest cornfields and to start a new life in California.

a) greateful
b) grateful
c) greatful

26.46. The #MeToo movement put employers on notice that they can no longer _____ workers with impunity, and supervisors who behave inappropriately in the workplace may be sued or even prosecuted.

a) harass
b) harrass
c) harras

26.47. "Every human has four endowments — self-awareness, conscience, _____ will, and creative imagination. These give us the ultimate human freedom...The power to choose, to respond, to change."—Stephen Covey

a) independant
b) independent
c) indapendant

26.48. Nietzsche observed: "All sciences are now under the obligation to prepare the ground for the future task of the philosopher, which is to solve the problem of value, to determine the true _____ of values."

a) hierarchy
b) higharchy
c) higherarchy
d) hirearchy

26.49. To adjust the _____ of the chair, simply lift up on the lever under the seat.

a) heigt
b) height
c) hight

26.50. You must have a driver's _____ to legally operate a vehicle on public streets.

a) lisense
b) lisence
c) license

26.51. The flood waters pose no _____ danger to any of the homes in the area.

a) imediate
b) immediete
c) immediate

26.52. The Pentagon has ordered enough vaccine to _____ soldiers who might be exposed to smallpox or anthrax in a war zone.

a) innoculate
b) inoculate
c) innocculate

26.53. A recent survey on dating found that over 75% of the respondents admitted that their dating partners had done something that made them _____ .

a) jelous
b) jealous
c) jelouse
d) jellous

26.54. "Nothing in all the world is more dangerous than sincere _____ and conscientious stupidity."—Martin Luther King Jr.

a) ignorence

b) ignoranse

c) ignorance

26.55. Rings, necklaces, and bracelets are common forms of _____.

a) jewlry

b) jewlery

c) jewelry

26.56. "The goal of education is not to increase the amount of _____ but to create the possibilities for a child to invent and discover, to create men who are capable of doing new things."—Jean Piaget

a) knowledge

b) knowlidge

c) knowlege

26.57. For some, writing is a _____ pastime, while for others, it is a compulsion.

a) leesure

b) leisure

c) leasure

26.58. David and Abby became lovers and best friends, and the _____ lasted for many years.

a) liaison

b) liason

c) laison

26.59. "The world is full of a lot of fear and a lot of negativity, and a lot of _____. I just think people need to start shifting into joy and happiness. As corny as it sounds, we need to make a shift." —Ellen DeGeneres

a) judgement

b) judgment

c) judgemint

26.60. The dealer informed Isabella that she should bring her car to the shop for an oil change and _____ every 5,000 miles.

a) maintenence

b) maintainence

c) maintenance

26.61. The carpenter's toolbox contained hammers, screwdrivers, a wrench, and _____ odds and ends

a) misellaneous

b) miscellaneous

26.62. Geometry, calculus and trigonometry are advanced forms of _____.

a) mathmatics

b) mathematics

c) mathematicks

26.63. Swords, daggers, and battle axes were common weapons in _____ times.

a) medieval

b) medeival

c) midieval

26.64. The taxi driver was able to deftly _____ his cab through rush hour traffic.

a) manuver

b) maneuver

c) maneuvore

26.65. The band's performance was _____ at best, and most of the crowd left after the first couple of songs.

a) mediocre

b) mediocer

c) mediocure

26.66. A greeting card or a snapshot can make the perfect _____ for a scrapbook.

a) momento

b) memento

c) mommento

26.67. A period of 100 years is a century, and a period of 1,000 years is a _____.

a) millenium

b) milennium

c) millennium

26.68. Household dust is typically made up of _____ various substances, including pollen, pet dander, dust mites and their excrement, decomposing insects, human hair, and skin flakes.

a) miniscule

b) minescule

c) minuscule

26.69. My sister in Texas has an adorable _____ poodle named Gracie.

a) miniture

b) miniature

c) minature

26.70. Shelby flashed her boyfriend a _____ smile, knowing that he would he amused by the practical joke she was about to play.

a) mischievous

b) mischievious

c) mischeivious

26.71. As the rain intensified, accompanied by thunder and lightning, a _____ shadow hovered in the dark alcove outside the industrialist's mansion.

a) mistereus

b) mysterious

c) mistereous

d) mystereous

26.72. Mr. Zhao was always cordial to his _____, but he instinctively disliked the man and did not trust him.

a) neighber

b) neighbor

c) naighbor

26.73. The scratch in the new table top is quite _____, and the table should be returned for a replacement.

a) noticable

b) noticible

c) noticeable

26.74. Melinda chose this _____ to announce that she and her fiancé had eloped.

a) occassion

b) occasion

c) ocassion

26.75. The hope for world _____ has become elusive in today's chaotic world.

a) peace

b) piece

c) pease

26.76. Fish falling from the sky was a bizarre and unexpected _____ that sent terrified villagers fleeing in all directions.

a) occurence

b) occurrance

c) occurrence

26.77. The priest renounced his ministry, declared himself a Buddhist, and embarked upon an _____ of discovery in Tibet.

a) odyssea

b) odyssea

c) odyssey

26.78. It takes planning and _____ to succeed. A bit of luck is helpful too.

a) perseverence

b) perseverance

c) perserverance

26.79. When the union voted to strike, the CEO made some _____ changes and fired all of his employees the next day.

a) personnel

b) personel

26.80. According to the Doomsday Clock, maintained by a group of the world's top atomic scientists, global events in 2018 have brought us closer than ever to the threat of _____ war.

a) nuclear
b) nuculear
c) nucleair

26.81. The birds that you are seeing out in the field are crows, sparrows, blue jays, and one large _____.

a) pidgeon
b) pigeon
c) pidgen

26.82. It might surprise you to know that the _____ and several other edible fruits are plant species in the rose family.

a) rasberry
b) raspberry
c) raspberry
d) raspbury

26.83. Which entrée on the menu do you _____?

a) reccommend
b) recommend
c) reccomend

26.84. "Even though it is more blessed to give than to _____, sometimes you need to be the object of someone else's compassion." —J. Earp

a) recieve
b) reseive
c) receive

26.85. The patient described her symptoms, and the doctor _____ her to a specialist.

a) referred
b) refered
c) refferred

26.86. Dining out at a _____ is fun, but it is more expensive than cooking meals at home.

a) restarant
b) resteraunt
c) restaurant

26.87. Despite the candidate's busy _____, she made time to visit a hospital, a school for disadvantaged children, and a nursing home.

a) scedule
b) schedule
c) schedulle

26.88. You cannot cut down that tree with _____, no matter how determined you might be.

a) scizzors
b) scissors
c) scissers

26.89. The drill _____ barked commands and made the new recruits march until they were about to collapse from exhaustion.

a) sergent
b) seargant
c) sergeant

26.90. Her son did a _____ job of washing the dinner dishes, even though he complained the whole time that his sister should have been doing the chore.

a) thorough
b) thurough
c) theurowe

26.91. The woman had toiled for years to lift herself out of poverty, and now, as she stood of the _____ of success, she knew that she would never forget her humble roots.

a) threshhold
b) threshold
c) threashold

26.92. The fighter jet passed _____ the clouds as it descended toward the runway.

a) thrue

b) threw

c) through

26.93. The _____ forecast for tomorrow predicts rain, hail and freezing temperatures.

a) wether

b) weather

c) whether

26.94. Angry that the fast food restaurant had run out of ketchup, the customer shouted obscenities and _____ his hamburger against the wall before storming out.

a) threw

b) thorough

c) through

26.95. That commercial was the _____ in less than fifteen minutes—it's no wonder so many people are turning off their TVs!

a) twealth

b) twelvth

c) twelfth

26.96. "Help! Why is _____ spelled like that?"—Blake Shelton

a) Wendsday

b) Wednesday

c) Wednsday

26.97. It has been said that we do not live our lives in a _____. Every thought we have, every action we take, has an effect on others around us.

a) vaccum

b) vaccume

c) vacuum

26.98. We will go for a drive to the mountains tomorrow, _____ it rains or not.

a) whether

b) weather

26.99. "So you're a little _____? Work it! A little different? Own it! Better to be a nerd than one of the herd!"—Mandy Hale

a) wierd

b) weard

c) weird

26.100. "The secret of freedom lies in educating people, whereas the secret of _____ is in keeping them ignorant." —Maximilien Robespierre

a) tyrany

b) tyranny

c) tireany

SECTION 6
Modern Grammar and Style

Quiz #27
Grammar and Style Rules

This quiz module is for readers of the 2018 Classic Edition. Questions are drawn from Chapter 7, *Style Rules for Better Writing*, which covers a variety of modern grammar and style rules not found in Strunk's first edition or the Strunk & White edition.

27.01. No matter how badly you want to write, no matter how deep your feelings, and no matter how exciting the ideas you want to share with others, if you don't know the basic rules of how to correctly form sentences and the relation of words to one another, your writing will lack coherency.

a) True
b) False

27.02. The author of *The Elements of Style* was _____.

a) a law professor at Yale
b) a literature professor at Harvard
c) a linguistics expert who worked for the U.S. Army
d) an English professor at Cornell University
e) None of these answers are correct.

27.03. When Prof. Strunk sold the publication rights for his grammar handout to a textbook publisher, he fully expected that it would be a best seller and, eventually, a classic.

a) True
b) False

27.04. Strunk's grammar book stresses the importance of writing grammatically correct prose and offers a blueprint that students and writers can follow to express their thoughts in a crisp, concise, effective manner.

a) True
b) False

27.05. The clearer your writing, the more likely it is that readers will fail to grasp the points you are trying to make.

a) True
b) False

27.06. To write correctly and effectively, a working grasp of the fundamentals of English grammar is not as important as possessing a rich vocabulary and a creative temperament.

a) True
b) False

27.07. Learning how to write correctly should be an easy challenge considering that the average person's vocabulary consists of a mere _____.

a) 2,000 words
b) 5,000 words
c) 6,500 words
d) 10,000 words

27.08. Many of the grammar rules in Strunk's book are as valid today as they were a century ago; but, the world has changed, and the English language has changed with it, making some of those rules obsolete.

a) True
b) False

27.09. Shakespeare's classic works contain about 15,000 different words, but more than _____ of those words are obsolete today.

a) 1,000
b) 6,000
c) 10,000

27.10. *The Elements of Style* was written by _____.

a) Allen Strunk
b) E.B. Strunk
c) William Strunk Jr.
d) William Strunk Sr.

27.11. The fundamental rules of grammar should be diligently followed so that you can express your thoughts and ideas in a clear and effective manner.

a) True

b) False

27.12. It has been said that the best way to learn to write is to write nothing until you have mastered the fundamentals of English grammar.

a) True

b) False

27.13. To understand the proper placement of words in sentences, it is important to know that all words in the English language are grouped into _____ categories, called "the parts of speech."

a) six

b) nine

c) eleven

d) thirteen

27.14. A _____ refers to the name of any person, place, or thing, which includes tangible objects and abstract concepts.

a) noun

b) pronoun

c) adjective

27.15. _____ nouns are formal names, as the names of people (John, Mary, Bob); places (London, Paris, Seattle); and countries (Canada, England, Mexico).

a) Common

b) Proper

c) Formal

d) Relative

27.16. English has four articles: *a* (or *an*), *the*, *this*, and *that*.

a) True

b) False

27.17. _____ denotes clear expression of thoughts conveyed in unequivocal language, so there is no misunderstanding of the idea that the writer wishes to express.

a) Perspicuity

b) Purity

c) Conformity

d) Precision

27.18. The _____ is the most important of the nine parts of speech, as all the rest are more or less dependent upon it.

a) verb

b) adjective

c) adverb

d) noun

27.19. An _____ is a word placed before a noun to show whether the noun is used in a particular or general sense.

a) adjective

b) article

c) adverb

d) interjection

27.20. Nouns fall into two categories: proper and _____.

a) improper

b) informal

c) common

d) plural

27.21. Nouns, adjectives, verbs, and adverbs become interjections when they are uttered as one-word exclamations.

a) True

b) False

27.22. Adverbs are typically used to express in one word what would otherwise require two or more words.

a) True

b) False

27.23. The article "a" is called the indefinite article because it does not refer to a particular person or thing but indicates the noun in its most general sense; for instance, *a man* can mean any man on the planet.

a) True

b) False

27.24. Consider these short phrases: a *black* dog, a *pretty* woman, a *cold* wind. The italicized words are _____.

a) nouns

b) adverbs

c) adjectives

27.25. Consider this sentence: "John gave *his* pen to James, and then *he* lent it to Jane to write *her* copy with *it*." The italicized words are:

a) nouns

b) pronouns

c) adverbs

27.26. Prepositions are usually placed before words whose connection or relation with other words they point out.

a) True

b) False

27.27. The singular _____ are: *I, me, my, mine; you, your, yours; he, him, his; she, her, hers;* and *it, its.*

a) nouns

b) articles

c) prepositions

d) pronouns

27.28. A _____ is a word that signifies action or the doing of something; or it may be a word that affirms, commands, or asks a question.

a) noun

b) verb

c) adjective

27.29. _____ refers to the use of proper English. It means writing without the use of slang words and expletives (except when writing fiction and then used sparingly), obsolete terms, foreign idioms, ambiguous expressions, and grammatically incorrect language.

a) Conformity

b) Perspicuity

c) Precision

d) Purity

27.30. The words *we, us, our, ours; you, your, yours;* and *they, them, their, theirs* are plural _____.

a) nouns

b) adjectives

c) pronouns

d) conjunctions

27.31. A/an _____ is a word used in place of a noun so that you don't have to repeat the same noun too often and fall into tedious repetition.

a) adjective

b) adverb

c) pronoun

d) article

27.32. Consider this sentence: "John *struck* the table with his fist." What is the italicized word?

a) a verb

b) an adverb

c) an interjection

d) a pronoun

27.33. An _____ is a word that modifies a verb, an adjective, or another adverb.

a) adjective

b) interjection

c) adverb

d) article

27.34. Consider this sentence: "He writes *well*." The italicized word is _____.

a) a verb

b) an adjective

c) a preposition

d) an adverb

27.35. You should never use active voice when you can use the passive.

a) True

b) False

27.36. Pronouns fall into two categories:

a) common and uncommon

b) formal and informal

c) singular and plural

d) common and proper

27.37. If it is possible to cut a word out, you should always cut it out.

a) True

b) False

27.38. Consider this sentence: "He is *remarkably* diligent." The italicized word is _____.

a) an adverb

b) an adjective

c) a verb

27.39. *Fire! Nonsense! Strange! No!* These words are:

a) prepositions

b) nouns

c) interjections

27.40. An _____ is a word that qualifies a noun, meaning it shows or points out some distinguishing mark or feature of the noun.

a) article

b) adverb

c) adjective

27.41. Consider this sentence: "She is *very* beautiful." The italicized word is _____.

a) a verb

b) an adverb

c) an adjective

d) a conjunction

27.42. The three essentials of effective writing in the English language are: purity, perspicuity, and precision.

a) True

b) False

27.43. A _____ connects words, clauses, and sentences together and shows the relation between them, as:

a) noun

b) preposition

c) verb

d) conjunction

27.44. Consider this sentence: "My hand is *on* the table." The italicized word is _____.

a) a preposition

b) a verb

c) an adverb

d) a conjunction

27.45. A/an _____ is a word that joins words, phrases, clauses, and sentences together.

a) preposition

b) article

c) adjective

d) conjunction

27.46. Consider this sentence: "John *and* James are close friends." The italicized word is _____.

a) a preposition

b) an adjective

c) a conjunction

27.47. Consider this sentence: "My father *and* mother arrived at the recital, *but* I did not see them." The italicized words are _____.

a) conjunctions

b) interjections

c) adjectives

d) prepositions

27.48. Consider this sentence: "I prefer apples *or* strawberries, *and* Tyrone prefers oranges." The italicized words are _____.

a) prepositions

b) interjections

c) conjunctions

d) articles

27.49. A/an _____ is a word that expresses surprise, shock, or some other sudden emotion.

a) preposition

b) interjection

c) interjection

d) adjective

27.50. This celebrated author offered poignant advice on grammar and style to writers in his discourse on *Politics and the English Language.*

a) Stephen King

b) Jonathan Swift

c) Charles Dickens

d) George Orwell

27.51. Consider this sentence: *"Ah!* There he comes." The italicized word is _____.

a) an interjection

b) a preposition

c) an adverb

27.52. _____ requires concise and exact expression, free from redundancy–a style that is clear and simple enough so that the reader can immediately comprehend the meaning of the writer's words.

a) Precision

b) Perspicuity

c) Parity

d) Purity

27.53. Consider this sentence: *"Alas!* What shall I do? *Ah!* There he comes!" The italicized words are _____.

a) conjunctions

b) prepositions

c) articles

d) interjections

27.54. The most common _____ are: *and, also; either, or; neither, nor; though, yet; but, however; for, that; because, since; therefore, wherefore, then,* and *if.*

a) interjections

b) adverbs

c) conjunctions

d) prepositions

27.55. _____ requires a style that is clear and concise, which means ambiguous words, words of double meaning, and words that might be construed in a sense different from that intended should be avoided.

a) Precision

b) Perspicuity

c) Purity

d) Parity

27.56. You should never use a foreign phrase, a scientific word, or jargon if you can think of an everyday English equivalent to use instead.

a) True

b) False

Section 7

Quiz Answers

Quiz #1 Answers

1.01. With a few exceptions, you should form the possessive singular of nouns by adding _____.

a) apostrophe + s (Bob's notebook)

1.02. Consider the use of possessive apostrophes in these phrases. Which form is written incorrectly?

c) Ross'es poems

1.03. You should use only an apostrophe and no "s" when writing the possessive form of Jesus, as in *Jesus' teachings*.

a) True

1.04. Consider the use of the possessive apostrophes in these phrases. Which phrase is written incorrectly?

b) Moses's teachings

1.05. Which sentence is written correctly?

a) The cat licked *its* paw.

1.06. Proper grammar might sometimes require that you use an apostrophe with the pronominal possessives *hers, theirs, yours,* and *oneself.*

b) False

1.07. Which of these expressions is written incorrectly?

c) the witchs' malice

1.08. Which sentence is written correctly?

c) The hat is *hers*.

1.09. Which phrase is written correctly?

b) Jesus' robe

1.10. Which expression is written incorrectly?

b) Isis's temple

1.11. An apostrophe is required after the pronominal possessive *its*.

b) False

1.12. Consider the use of possessive apostrophes in these constructions. Which sentence is written correctly?

d) They believe the land is *theirs*, but they are wrong.

1.13. Which sentence is written correctly?

b) The choice is *yours*, so decide quickly.

Quiz #2 Answers

2.01. A comma placed before a conjunction in a series of three or more terms is called _____.

e) None of these answers are correct.

2.02. In business firm names, you should omit the last comma in a series of names, as *Brown, Shipley & Co.*

a) True

2.03. Consider the use of commas in the following business name, where Joe Allen, Kelsey Jones, and Brad Smith are the owners. Which form is written correctly?

c) Allen, Jones, Smith & Co.

2.04. Which phrase uses a serial comma correctly?

b) red, white, and blue

2.05. Another name for a serial comma is _____.

a) an Oxford comma

2.06. Assume that the use of serial commas is required in your writing. Which phrase is written correctly?

d) gold, silver, or copper

2.07. Which sentence uses the serial comma correctly?

a) He opened the letter, read it, and discarded it.

2.08. Which sentence uses the serial comma correctly?

c) Mary packed a turkey sandwich, one orange, two apples, and a cookie in her son's lunch pail.

Quiz #3 Answers

3.01. Parenthetical expressions usually should be set off by commas.

a) True

3.02. Which sentence uses commas correctly to mark off a parenthetical phrase?

c) Sheila's husband, Captain Garcia, paid us a visit today.

3.03. Read this sentence and choose the answer that best defines the italicized words: "The best way to see a country, *unless you are pressed for time*, is to travel on foot."

d) a parenthetical phrase

3.04. Which of these sentences uses commas correctly to mark off a parenthetical phrase?

a) My father, I am happy to say, has now fully recovered.

3.05. Sometimes it is hard to decide whether a single word, such as "however," or a brief phrase, is or is not parenthetical.

a) True

3.06. With a parenthetical phrase, if the interruption to the flow of the sentence is slight, it is acceptable to omit the offsetting commas.

a) True

3.07. When a parenthetical expression is preceded by a conjunction, you should _____.

b) Write the first comma before the conjunction.

3.08. In a sentence with a parenthetical phrase, it is acceptable to insert the opening comma, and omit the closing comma, if it improves the flow of the passage.

b) False

3.09. These sentences contain a parenthetical phrase. Which sentence is written correctly?

c) He saw us coming, and unaware that we had learned of his treachery, greeted us with a smile.

3.10. A parenthetical expression is a clause or phrase that is inserted within another clause or phrase.

a) True

3.11. If a sentence contains a parenthetical phrase, and you delete that phrase, you will no longer have a complete sentence.

b) False

3.12. Consider the parenthetical phrase in these sentences. Which is written correctly?

c) The candidate who best meets these requirements will be hired for the job.

3.13. Which phrase is punctuated correctly?

d) February to July, 2016

3.14. Which date is punctuated correctly?

b) April 6, 2017

3.15. Which date is punctuated correctly?

a) Monday, November 11, 2018

3.16. These constructions contain a parenthetical expression. Which is written correctly?

d) The day will come when you will admit your mistake.

Quiz #4 Answers

4.01. A comma should be placed before a conjunction that introduces a coordinate clause.

a) True

4.02. In these sentences, a conjunction introduces a coordinate clause requiring a comma. Which sentence is written correctly?

b) The early records of the city have disappeared, and the story of its first years can no longer be reconstructed.

4.03. Two-part sentences of which the second member is introduced by *as* (in the sense of *because*), *for, or, nor,* and *while* (in the sense of *and at the same time*) require a comma after the conjunction.

b) False

4.04. Strunk advises that it is not necessarily good style to make all your sentences short and brief. An occasional loose sentence prevents your style from becoming too formal and gives the reader a bit of relief.

a) True

4.05. If a dependent clause, or an introductory phrase that must be set off by a comma, precedes a second independent clause, a comma is required after the conjunction.

b) False

4.06. In these constructions, a conjunction introduces a coordinate clause. Which sentence is written correctly?

c) The situation at the coal mine is perilous, but there is still one chance of escape.

4.07. Which sentence is punctuated correctly?

d) The situation is perilous, but if we are prepared to act promptly, we may still escape.

4.08. In a two-part sentence, if the second member is introduced by an adverb, you should use a semicolon rather than a comma to connect the two parts.

a) True

4.09. In these constructions, the subject is the same for both clauses and is expressed only once. Which is written correctly?

b) I have heard his arguments, but am still unconvinced.

4.10. In the following sentences, the subject is the same for both clauses and is expressed only once. Which sentence is written correctly?

c) He has had several years' experience and is thoroughly competent.

4.11. The connectives *so* and *yet* may be used either as adverbs or as conjunctions, where the second clause is intended to be coordinate or subordinate; so, using either a comma or a semicolon may be appropriate.

a) True

4.12. When the subject is the same for both clauses and is expressed only once, a comma is not required if the connective is *but*.

b) False

4.13. When the subject is the same for both clauses and is expressed only once, if the connective is *and*, you should omit the comma if the relation between the two statements is close or immediate.

a) True

Quiz #5 Answers

5.01. It is acceptable to break a compound sentence into two shorter elements, where both form complete sentences, but doing so often results in choppy wording.

a) True

5.02. You may break sentences in two when one element or the other does not form a complete sentence, as long as you mark the break with a period, as in this example: "I met Kate on a cruise in June. Sailing from San Diego to Cancun."

b) False

5.03. Which sentence is punctuated correctly?

b) I met Kate on a cruise last year, sailing from San Diego to Cancun.

5.04. It is acceptable to make an emphatic word or expression serve the purpose of a sentence and to punctuate it accordingly, as: "Again and again he called out. No reply."

a) True

Quiz #6 Answers

6.01. If two or more clauses, grammatically complete and not joined by a conjunction, are written to form a compound sentence, the proper punctuation mark is a semicolon.

a) True

6.02. The following sentences contain two complete clauses not joined by a conjunction. Which sentence is written incorrectly?

c) Stevenson's romances are entertaining, they are full of exciting adventures.

6.03. The following sentences contain two complete clauses joined by a conjunction. Which sentence is written correctly?

a) Stevenson's romances are entertaining, for they are full of exciting adventures.

6.04. If the second clause in a sentence containing two complete clauses is preceded by an adverb, such as *accordingly, besides, then, therefore,* or *thus*, and not by a conjunction, the semicolon is not required.

b) False

6.05. The following sentences contain two complete clauses not joined by a conjunction. Which sentence is not written correctly?

b) It is half past five; and we can't reach town before dark.

6.06. If a conjunction is inserted between two complete clauses rather than a semicolon, the correct punctuation mark to use is a _____.

a) comma

6.07. These sentences contain two complete clauses joined by a conjunction. Which is not written correctly?

c) It is nearly half past five, we cannot reach town before the sun goes down.

6.08. Which sentence is written correctly?

b) The car stopped, the driver fled, the police pursued.

6.09. If a sentence consists of two complete clauses, and the two are very short and alike in form, it is usually acceptable to use a comma, as, "Anya complains, Lorena acts."

a) True

6.10. Which sentence is written correctly?

c) The door swung open, the gun fired, the intruder fled.

Quiz #7 Answers

7.01. A participial phrase at the beginning of a sentence may refer to the grammatical subject or to any other noun in the sentence.

b) False

7.02. Participial phrases preceded by a conjunction or a preposition, nouns in apposition, adjectives, and adjective phrases must always refer to the grammatical subject if they begin the sentence.

a) True

7.03. Which construction is grammatically preferable?

b) When he arrived in Chicago, David's friends met him at the station.

7.04. Which construction is grammatically preferable?

a) A courageous soldier, Capt. Jones was entrusted with the defense of the city.

7.05. Which sentence is written correctly?

c) Young and inexperienced, I thought the task easy.

7.06. Which form is grammatically preferable?

c) Without a friend to counsel him, he found the temptation irresistible.

7.07. Which sentence is written correctly?

a) Being in a dilapidated condition, the house was for sale very cheap.

7.08. Which sentence is written correctly?

b) Wondering in dismay what to do next, I heard the clock strike twelve.

Quiz #8 Answers

8.01. A paragraph should be the basic unit of composition, and each paragraph should express a complete thought.

a) True

8.02. If the subject on which you are writing is of a trivial nature, or if you intend to treat it very briefly, you should still subdivide it into multiple paragraphs, and some of those paragraphs may consist of just one sentence.

b) False

8.03. For a subject that is complex and consists of several or more topics, it is acceptable to combine multiple topics into a single paragraph to save space and help readers move through your writing quickly.

b) False

8.04. The beginning of each paragraph is a signal to the reader that _____.

c) A new step in the development of the subject has been reached.

8.05. A brief description, a brief book review or account of a single incident, a narrative that merely outlines an action, the expressing of a single idea, any one of these is best written in a single paragraph.

a) True

8.06. A report on a poem, written for a literature class, might typically consist of just one paragraph.

b) False

8.07. A single sentence, with a few exceptions, should not be written as a paragraph.

a) True

8.08. For sentences of transition, and in textbooks, guides, and other works in which many topics are treated briefly, it is not acceptable to write a single sentence as a paragraph.

b) False

8.09. In dialogue, each speech, even if only a single word, is a paragraph by itself. In other words, a new paragraph begins with each change of speaker.

a) True

Quiz #9 Answers

9.01. Beginning each paragraph with a topic sentence will allow readers to discover the purpose of each paragraph as they begin to read it, and to retain this purpose in mind as they end it.

a) True

9.02. In a well-structured paragraph, the topic sentence comes at or near the beginning; the succeeding sentences either emphasize the thought of the topic sentence or state some important consequence; and the final sentence explains, establishes, or develops the statement made in the topic sentence.

b) False

9.03. You should avoid ending a paragraph with an unimportant detail or a digression.

a) True

9.04. If a paragraph forms part of a larger composition, its relation to what precedes, or its function as a part of the whole, may need to be expressed. This can be done sometimes by a mere word or phrase (*again; therefore; for the same reason*) in the topic sentence.

a) True

Quiz #10 Answers

10.01. The active voice is usually more direct and vigorous than the passive voice.

a) True

10.02. Which form is written in active voice?

a) I shall always remember my first visit to Paris.

10.03. Although writing in active voice should be heavily favored, sometimes a sentence will read better if written in passive voice, or using passive voice may even be necessary.

a) True

10.04. Which construction is grammatically preferable in a paragraph discussing the dramatists of the Restoration?

b) The dramatists of the Restoration are little esteemed today.

10.05. Which construction is grammatically preferable in a paragraph discussing the tastes of modern readers?

b) Modern readers have little esteem for the dramatists of the Restoration.

10.06. As a rule, your prose will be clearer and more concrete if you favor constructions in which one passive depends directly upon another.

b) False

10.07. If your aim is to avoid making one passive depend directly on another, which construction should you use?

b) It has been proved that he was seen entering the room.

10.08. A common fault is to use as the subject of a passive construction a noun that expresses the entire action and leaves to the verb no function other than completing the sentence.

a) True

10.09. Which construction contains a grammar fault that should be avoided?

a) Confirmation of these reports cannot be obtained.

10.10. Which sentence avoids passive construction of a noun that expresses the entire action and leaves the verb with no function other than completing the sentence?

b) This region was surveyed in 1900.

10.11. Which sentence avoids passive construction of a noun that expresses the entire action and leaves the verb with no function other than completing the sentence?

b) The army was rapidly mobilized.

10.12. Many bland descriptive sentences can be made lively and more emphatic by substituting a verb in the active voice for some such perfunctory expression as *there is*, or *could be heard*.

a) True

10.13. The habitual use of passive voice makes for forcible writing. This is true not only in narrative mainly concerned with action, but in writing of any kind.

b) False

10.14. Which sentence substitutes a verb in the active voice to make the passage interesting or emphatic?

c) Somewhere in the house a guitar hummed sleepily.

10.15. Which sentence substitutes a verb in the active voice to make the passage interesting or emphatic?

c) Dead leaves covered the ground.

10.16. Which construction is grammatically preferable?

b) Failing health compelled him to leave college.

Quiz #11 Answers

11.01. You should avoid tame, colorless, non-committal language, and make definite assertions in your writing.

a) True

11.02. The word *not* is inherently weak. Consciously or unconsciously, the reader is dissatisfied with being told only what is not; he wishes to be told what is. Therefore, as a rule, it is better to express even a negative in positive form.

a) True

11.03. Which sentence is grammatically better?

b) He usually came late.

11.04. Which sentence is written correctly?

a) He thought the study of Latin useless.

11.05. Which construction is stronger?

b) Dishonest

11.06. Strunk advises that you should use *not* as a means of denial or evasion, and never in antithesis.

b) False

11.07. Which sentence uses Strunk's grammar rules more effectively?

b) The women in *The Taming of the Shrew* are unattractive. Katharine is disagreeable, Bianca insignificant.

11.08. Negative words other than *not* are usually strong.

a) True

11.09. Which construction is weaker?

a) Did not remember

11.10. Which construction is stronger?

b) Distrusted

Quiz #12 Answers

12.01. A writer is well advised to prefer the specific to the general, the definite to the vague, the concrete to the abstract.

a) True

12.02. Which construction is more definite and specific?

b) It rained every day for a week.

12.03. Which construction is more definite and specific?

a) He grinned as he pocketed the coin.

12.04. Prose, in particular narrative and descriptive prose, is made vivid by definite and concrete words that evoke mental pictures in the reader's mind.

a) True

12.05. Which construction is more definite and specific?

b) All who have tried surf riding agree that it is most exhilarating.

Quiz #13 Answers

13.01. If you want to write lively and exemplary prose, you should make all your sentences short, use simple words, and make every word tell.

b) False

13.02. Which sentence should be rewritten to eliminate word clutter?

c) Owing to the fact that Marcus failed to pay his bill, his electricity was shut off.

13.03. Prof. Strunk advises that vigorous writing is concise, and a sentence should contain no unnecessary words, a paragraph no unnecessary sentences.

a) True

13.04. Which expression is less concise?

a) The question as to whether

13.05. Which expression is more concise?

b) No doubt

13.06. Which sentence contains word clutter?

b) Used for fuel purposes

13.07. Which expression is more concise?

a) He

13.08. Which sentence should be rewritten to eliminate word clutter?

b) In spite of the fact that I left early, I was still late for my appointment.

13.09. Which phrase is less concise?

a) In a hasty manner

13.10. Which phrase is more concise?

b) This subject

13.11. Which sentence is free of word clutter?

a) His story is strange.

13.12. The expression *the fact that* should be deleted from every sentence in which it occurs.

a) True

13.13. Which sentence should be rewritten to avoid word clutter?

a) We call your attention to the fact that your taxes are delinquent.

13.14. Which construction is grammatically preferable?

b) His failure on the first attempt simply inspired him to try harder.

13.15. *Who is, which was,* and the like are often superfluous and should be written out of sentences.

a) True

13.16. Which sentence should be rewritten to avoid word clutter?

b) I was unaware of the fact that Ariana was born in Italy.

13.17. Which sentence reflects better grammar?

b) My arrival two hours late was cause for concern.

13.18. Which construction is more concise?

a) His brother, a member of the same firm

13.19. Which construction is grammatically preferable?

b) Trafalgar, Nelson's last battle

13.20. A common violation of conciseness is presenting a single complex idea, step by step, in a series of sentences or independent clauses that might be more effectively combined into one.

a) True

Quiz #14 Answers

14.01. A "loose" sentence is a particular type consisting of two coordinate clauses, the second introduced by a conjunction or relative.

a) True

14.02. A series of loose sentences might be acceptable in writing but will likely become monotonous.

a) True

14.03. If you find that you have written a series of loose sentences, you should:

b) Recast at least enough of them to remove the monotony.

Quiz #15 Answers

15.01. The principle of "parallel construction" requires that expressions of similar content and function should be outwardly similar.

a) True

15.02. Which phrase expresses coordinate ideas correctly?

b) The French, the Italians, the Spanish, and the Greeks

15.03. Which of these sentences is written correctly?

b) Formerly, science was taught by the text-book method; now it is taught by the laboratory method.

15.04. An article or a preposition that applies to all the members of a series must either be used only before the first term or else be repeated before each term.

a) True

15.05. The expressions *both, and; not, but; not only, but also; either, or; first, second, third*; and the like are called:

c) Correlative expressions

15.06. Which sentence is written incorrectly because it relies on unlike constructions?

b) It was both a long ceremony and very tedious.

15.07. Correlative expressions should be followed by the same grammatical construction, that is, by the same part of speech, such as "both Aisha and I" and "not silk, but a cheap substitute."

a) True

15.08. Which construction is grammatically incorrect?

a) In spring, summer, and in winter

15.09. Which sentence is flawed because it relies on unlike constructions?

a) My objections are, first, the injustice of the measure; second, that it is unconstitutional.

15.10. Which sentence is written correctly?

a) A time not for words, but for action.

15.11. Which sentence is written incorrectly?

b) Either you must grant his request or incur his ill will.

Quiz #16 Answers

16.01. In a sentence, you should try to bring together the words, and groups of words, that are related in thought, and keep apart those which are not so related.

a) True

16.02. According to modern grammar rules, it is often acceptable to start a sentence with "There is" or a similar form of the expression.

b) False

16.03. Modifiers should come, if possible, next to the word they modify.

a) True

16.04. Which sentence is better grammar?

b) In the fifth book of *The Excursion*, Wordsworth gives a minute description of this church.

16.05. Which construction reflects better grammar?

b) By treatment in a Bessemer converter, cast iron is changed into steel.

16.06. Usually, a relative pronoun should come immediately _____.

c) after its antecedent

16.07. Which form is grammatically preferable?

b) He published in *Harper's Magazine* three articles about his adventures in Spain.

16.08. Which passage is written correctly?

a) This is a portrait of Benjamin Harrison, grandson of William Henry Harrison. He became President in 1889.

16.09. Which sentence is less ambiguous?

a) He found only two mistakes.

16.10. Which sentence is preferable?

b) In his eye was a look that boded mischief.

16.11. A noun in apposition should never come between antecedent and relative, because in such a combination ambiguity can arise.

b) False

16.12. If several expressions modify the same word, they should be so arranged to avoid ambiguity or confusing the reader.

a) True

16.13. Which passage is less ambiguous?

a) On Tuesday at eight P. M., Major R. E. Joyce will give in Bailey Hall a lecture on "My Experiences in Mesopotamia." The public is invited.

16.14. Which sentence is less ambiguous?

b) Not all the members were present.

Quiz #17 Answers

17.01. In summarizing a poem, story, or novel, you should use the past tense, since the poem was written in the past, though you may use present tense if you prefer.

b) False

17.02. Prof. Strunk advises that in summarizing the action of a drama, you should always use the _____.

c) present tense

17.03. As a general rule, it is good practice to shift from one tense to another in your writing, as it gives your prose a sense of being fresh, and it will hold your reader's interest.

b) False

17.04. In writing a summary, you should aim to write an orderly discussion supported by evidence, not a summary with occasional comment.

a) True

17.05. In presenting the statements or the thought of someone else, as in summarizing an essay or reporting a speech, you should avoid intercalating such expressions as "he said," "he stated," "the speaker added," "the author also thinks," and the like.

a) True

17.06. When summarizing a poem, a story, or a novel, whichever tense is used in the summary, a past tense in indirect discourse or in indirect question should be changed to present tense.

b) False

17.07. In newspapers and in many kinds of textbooks, summaries of one kind or another may be indispensable, and it is a useful exercise for children in primary schools to retell a story in their own words. But in the criticism or interpretation of literature, you should be careful to avoid dropping into summary.

a) True

Quiz #18 Answers

18.01. The proper place in a sentence for the word, or group of words, which you want to make most prominent is usually _____.

a) the end

18.02. Which sentence better emphasizes the thought that the writer is trying to establish as the most prominent?

b) Humanity, since that time, has advanced in many other ways, but it has hardly advanced in fortitude.

18.03. Besides the end of a sentence, the other prominent position in a sentence is the beginning, and any element in the sentence, other than the subject, may become emphatic when placed first.

a) True

18.04. The word or group of words entitled to a position of prominence in a sentence is usually the logical predicate.

a) True

18.05. Which sentence better emphasizes the thought that the writer is trying to establish as the most prominent?

b) Because of its hardness, this steel is principally used in making razors.

18.06. The principle that the proper place for what is to be made most prominent is the end applies equally to the words of a sentence, to the sentences of a paragraph, and to the paragraphs of a composition.

a) True

Quiz #19 Answers

19.01. Prof. Strunk advises that you should leave a blank line after the title or heading of a manuscript, and on subsequent pages, you should...

c) begin typing on the first line

19.02. In a scholarly work requiring exact references, titles that occur frequently should be abbreviated and the full forms given in the index or in a preface at the beginning.

b) False

19.03. You should omit the words *act, scene, line, book, page, volume* in references to particular works, except when referring to only one of them.

a) True

19.04. As a general practice, you should give references in the body of the sentence, not in parenthesis or in footnotes.

b) False

Quiz #20 Answers

20.01. Colloquialisms and slang do not require quotation marks, unless such marks would normally be required, such as to set off dialogue or a quoted excerpt.

a) True

20.02. Quotations introduced by the word *that* are regarded as indirect discourse and should be enclosed in quotation marks.

b) False

20.03. Consider the use of quotation marks and commas in these sentences. Which passage is written correctly?

c) I recall the maxim of La Rochefoucauld, "Gratitude is a lively sense of benefits to come."

20.04. Consider the use of quotation marks and commas in these sentences. Which passage is written correctly?

d) Aristotle says, "Art is an imitation of nature."

20.05. Quotations grammatically in apposition, or the direct objects of verbs, should be preceded by a comma and enclosed in quotation marks.

a) True

20.06. Consider the indirect quotation in these passages. Which sentence is written correctly?

b) Keats declares that beauty is truth, truth beauty.

20.07. Proverbial expressions and familiar phrases of literary origin require quotation marks.

b) False

20.08. Consider the proverbial expression used in these constructions. Which sentence is written correctly?

d) These are the times that try men's souls.

20.09. Consider the phrase used in the following constructions. Which sentence is written correctly?

c) He lives far from the madding crowd.

Quiz #21 Answers

21.01. How would you break "knowledge" at the end of a line?

a) know-ledge

21.02. How would you break "Shakespeare" at the end of a line?

c) Shake-speare

21.03. How would you break "describe" at the end of a line?

b) de-scribe

21.04. How would you break "atmosphere" at the end of a line?

b) atmos-phere

21.05. Using Strunk's "divide on the vowel" rule, how would you break "edible" at the end of a line?

a) edi-ble

21.06. Using Strunk's "divide on the vowel" rule, how would you break "proposition" at the end of a line?

c) propo-sition

21.07. How would you break "ordinary" at the end of a line?

b) ordi-nary

21.08. How would you break "religious" at the end of a line?

a) reli-gious

21.09. How would you break "opponents" at the end of a line?

c) oppo-nents

21.10. How would you break "regular" at the end of a line?

c) regu-lar

21.11. How would you break "classification" at the end of a line?

b) classi-fication

21.12. How would you break "decorative" at the end of a line?

a) deco-rative

21.13. How would you break "president" at the end of a line?

a) presi-dent

21.14. How would you break "Apennines" at the end of a line?

b) Apen-nines

21.15. How would you break "Cincinnati" at the end of a line?

b) Cincin-nati

21.16. How would you break "referring" at the end of a line?

a) refer-ring

21.17. How would you break "telling" at the end of a line?

b) tell-ing

21.18. How would you break "fortune" at the end of a line?

b) for-tune

21.19. How would you break "picture" at the end of a line?

a) pic-ture

21.20. How would you break "single" at the end of a line?

c) sin-gle

21.21. How would you break "illustration" at the end of a line?

b) illus-tration

21.22. How would you break "substantial" at the end of a line?

c) substan-tial

21.23. How would you break "instruction" at the end of a line?

a) instruc-tion

21.24. How would you break "suggestion" at the end of a line?

c) sugges-tion

21.25. How would you break "incendiary" at the end of a line?

b) incen-diary

Quiz #22 Answers

22.01. Which sentence is written correctly?

c) The patient says that she is feeling *all right* today.

22.02. *Can* and *may* have the same meaning, and may be used interchangeably.

b) False

22.03. Which phrase is written correctly?

b) I have no doubt that...

22.04. Which sentence is written correctly?

a) Many of the rooms were poorly ventilated.

22.05. The following sentences compare the quality of one essay to another. Which sentence is grammatically flawed?

b) Laura's essay is as good or better than his.

22.06. Which sentence is written correctly?

a) Whether the assassin is convicted will depend on the evidence presented.

22.07. Which phrase is written correctly?

a) He could not help seeing that...

22.08. Which sentence is written correctly?

b) Few mistakes have been made.

22.09. *Claim* is not a proper substitute for *declare, charge,* or *maintain.*

a) True

22.10. The word *certainly* is a good choice in a sentence where you want to intensify the point being made, just as the word *very* is a good choice to emphasize your point.

b) False

22.11. Which passage uses the word *but* more effectively?

b) America seemed wholly unprepared for war, *but* she had vast resources. Within a year she had created an army of four million men.

22.12. Which form is better grammar?

c) I consider him thoroughly competent.

22.13. When Strunk wrote *The Elements of Style* in the early 1900s, his advice was to treat *data* as a plural noun. Today, *data* is widely used as both singular and plural.

a) True

22.14. Which sentence is written correctly?

c) The red Ford is *different from* the other cars on the lot.

22.15. Which sentence is written correctly?

a) He claimed to be the sole surviving heir.

22.16. Which statement accurately describes the division of plays and poems?

a) Plays are *divided into* acts, but poems are *composed of* stanzas.

22.17. Which sentence describing Mario's carelessness is grammatically correct?

c) Mario lost the game *because of* his own carelessness.

22.18. It is appropriate to use the expression *due to* in some constructions, but not others. With that in mind, which sentence is written incorrectly?

c) Franco slipped and fell *due to* his own carelessness.

22.19. Prof. Strunk advises that *folk* is a collective noun, equivalent to *people*, and it denotes plural form.

b) False

22.20. Used as a noun, *affect* means "result," and as a verb, it means to "bring about, accomplish."

b) False

22.21. As a verb, *effect* means "to produce something or cause something to occur," and *affect* means "to influence."

a) True

22.22. Consider the use of *effect* and *affect* in these phrases and identify the grammatically flawed construction.

c) broad *affects* can be seen

22.23. *Etc.* is equivalent to "and the rest," "and so forth." It typically follows a series of items in a list and indicates more items could have been listed.

a) True

22.24. You should never use *etc.* at the end of a list introduced by *such as, for example,* or any similar expression.

a) True

22.25. The words *less* and *fewer* mean the same and can be used interchangeably.

b) False

22.26. Which form reflects better grammar?

b) He is very ambitious.

22.27. Sometimes *factor* is appropriate to use in a sentence; other times, it muddles the writer's point and should not be used. Which sentence reflects better grammar?

a) He won the match by being better trained.

22.28. Which form reflects better grammar?

b) Heavy artillery has played a constantly larger part in deciding battles.

22.29. Which sentence contains flawed grammar that should never appear in academic or formal writing?

c) Those dogs have got fleas from being outdoors.

22.30. Which form reflects better grammar?

b) I have always wanted to visit Spain.

22.31. Consider the words *less* and *fewer* in these passages and identify the correctly written sentence.

b) He had *fewer* men than in the previous campaign

22.32. Which sentence is most likely to escape criticism from the Grammar Police?

c) Prince Khalid, who it is expected will soon visit America, was once poor.

22.33. Use *fact* only for matters that can directly verified, not matters of judgment. That a certain event happened on a given date is a fact; but such conclusions as that the climate of California is delightful or that the cost of living is sky-high these days, however incontestable they may be, are not properly facts.

a) True

22.34. Consider the use of *rather* and *kind of* in these constructions and choose the correctly written sentence.

a) David was *rather* disappointed when his girlfriend told him that she had to work Saturday night.

22.35. *Line* used in the sense of *course of procedure, conduct, thought,* is allowable, but has been so much overworked, especially in the phrase *along these lines*, that it should be discarded entirely.

a) True

22.36. *Less* refers to number, and *fewer* refers to quantity.

b) False

22.37. "Jacob's troubles are less than mine" means that Jacob's troubles are not so great as mine.

a) True

22.38. Consider the use of *rather, kind of,* and *sort of* in these sentences and choose the grammatically correct form.

b) Amber is a kind of fossil resin.

22.39. The word *like* is often misused for *as*. Which sentence is written correctly?

b) We spent the evening *as* in the old days.

22.40. The word *as* governs nouns and pronouns. Before phrases and clauses, the equivalent word is *like*.

b) False

22.41. Which form is grammatically correct?

b) Mr. B. also spoke, to the same effect.

22.42. Which sentence is written correctly?

a) He is studying French literature.

22.43. Which phrase is written correctly?

b) a flood of abuse

22.44. Consider the use of *like* and *as* in these sentences and choose the correct form.

a) He thought *as* I did.

22.45. Which phrase is written correctly?

b) almost dead with fatigue

22.46. *Most* and *almost* are synonymous and can be used interchangeably.

b) False

22.47. Consider the use of *most* and *almost* in these sentences and choose the correct form.

a) *Almost* everybody at the party had too much to drink.

22.48. Which sentence is written correctly?

c) Joshua was optimistic *almost all the time.*

22.49. Which sentence is written correctly?

b) The army engaged in hostile acts.

22.50. You should avoid beginning paragraphs with *one of the most*, as, "One of the most interesting developments of modern science..." as this expression is threadbare.

a) True

22.51. Which form is grammatically correct?

b) Switzerland is *among the most* beautiful countries of Europe.

22.52. Consider the use of the singular *has* and plural *have* in these phrases and select the correctly written sentence.

b) One of the ablest men that *have* attacked this problem

22.53. Strunk's rule of thumb is that any clumsily worded sentence should be recast. Similarly, if the use of the possessive is awkward or impossible, the sentence should be recast. With these rules in mind, which phrase should be rewritten?

a) In the event of a reconsideration of the whole matter's becoming necessary

22.54. Usually, the words *respective* and *respectively* can be omitted from a sentence without altering its meaning.

a) True

22.55. Identify the grammatically flawed sentence in need of rewriting.

c) There was great dissatisfaction with the decision of the judge being favorable to the company.

22.56. *Possess* should not be used as a mere substitute for *have* or *own*.

a) True

22.57. *The people* is a political term, not to be confused with *the public*. From the people comes political support or opposition; from the public comes artistic appreciation or commercial patronage.

a) True

22.58. Which construction is grammatically preferable?

b) He had great courage.

22.59. Which form is preferable?

b) He owned

22.60. Which construction should you avoid in writing?

a) popular with the student body

22.61. Which form is preferable?

b) Works of fiction are listed under the names of their authors.

22.62. Which of these sentences reflect better grammar?

a) The one-mile and two-mile runs were won by Jones and by Cummings.

22.63. For the following conditional statement in first person, which form is correct?

b) I should not have succeeded without his help.

22.64. It is good practice to use *state* as a substitute for *say* or *remark*.

b) False

22.65. If we adhere to Strunk's rules on the proper use of *state* and *say* or *remark*, only one of these sentences is written correctly. Identify that sentence.

d) He refused to state his objections.

22.66. It is better to use *student body* than *students* as it sounds more official.

b) False

22.67. As a general rule, writers should use *while* only with strict literalness, in the sense of *during the time that*.

a) True

22.68. Which construction reflects better grammar?

a) The students passed the budget resolution.

22.69. *Shall* is widely used today in technical and academic writing.

b) False

22.70. Which sentence should be rewritten?

b) The office and salesrooms are on the ground floor, while the rest of the building is devoted to manufacturing.

22.71. The word *very* should be used sparingly because it is overused and other strong words can be substituted for better effect.

a) True

22.72. You should avoid the indiscriminate use of *while* in place of *and*, *but*, and *although*.

a) True

22.73. Strunk advises that the phrase *thanking you in advance* should be avoided in correspondence because:

c) It sounds as if the writer meant, "It will not be worth my while to write to you again."

22.74. Many writers use *while* as a substitute for *and* or *but;* in such uses, however, it is best replaced by a semicolon.

a) True

22.75. Which sentence is written correctly?

b) Although the temperature may reach 95 degrees Fahrenheit in the daytime, the nights are often chilly.

22.76. The word *worthwhile* is overworked as a term of vague approval (and when used with *not,* of disapproval). It should only be used with nouns, as, "That sci-fi novel is a worthwhile book."

b) False

22.77. Which form is written correctly?

b) His books are not worth reading.

22.78. The use of *worthwhile* before a noun, as in "a worthwhile story," is bad grammar and should be avoided.

a) True

Quiz #23 Answers

23.01. Some writers resort to using *lose out* as a more emphatic expression than *lose*, but it is actually less so because of its commonness.

a) True

23.02. If you follow Prof. Strunk's advice on using the word *dependable*, which construction is the better choice?

b) Martha is a *reliable* friend who always has a bright smile or a kind word.

23.03. Which construction does a better job of avoiding word clutter?

b) Dayton has adopted government by commission.

23.04. Considering Strunk's advice on using the word *dependable*, which construction is the better choice?

a) I am quite certain Jose is trustworthy and would never steal from the cash drawer.

23.05. *Don't* is a contraction that can be written in place of either *do not* or *does not*.

b) False

23.06. In American English, *fix* should only be used in technical and other formal writing when you mean:

b) fasten, make firm or immovable, etc.

23.07. Which sentence is written correctly?

b) The Gonzales family lives in the neighboring community.

23.08. According to Prof. Strunk, *ofttimes* and *oftentimes* are archaic forms, and *often* should be substituted instead.

a) True

23.09. It's acceptable and sometimes preferable to use "so" as an intensifier; for example, *so good, so warm*.

b) False

23.10. When you need to write out a number, which form is grammatically preferable:

c) one hundred and twenty hours

23.11. Which construction effectively avoids word clutter?

b) The army relies on dormitories to house troops during boot camp training.

23.12. When it comes to writing about a candidate expressing an opinion, which sentence contains faulty grammar?

b) The candidate did not hesitate to express his viewpoint on immigration.

23.13. Which sentence is written correctly?

b) His brother, *who* he said would send him the money, mysteriously disappeared.

23.14. Which construction is grammatically correct?

a) The man *whom* he thought was his friend

23.15. Which construction is grammatically correct?

a) The man *who* he thought was his friend

Quiz #24 Answers

24.01. The words *irritate* and *aggravate* mean the same and may be used interchangeably.

b) False

24.02. Which sentence uses the italicized word correctly?

a) The lonely old woman often *alluded* to the fact that her son never had time to visit her.

24.03. Which sentence uses the italicized word correctly?

b) The new blood pressure medication is more expensive, and it *aggravates* her vertigo.

24.04. Which sentence uses the italicized word correctly?

a) That scratchy fabric *irritates* Julia's skin.

24.05. Which sentence is written correctly?

a) The burglar *eluded* police by fleeing into a dark alley.

24.06. Which sentence uses the italicized word correctly?

b) The child's crying is *irritating* to him.

24.07. Which sentence is written correctly?

a) No matter how many books the writer has published, success still *eludes* him.

24.08. Which sentence uses the italicized word correctly?

c) The voters saw through the scheme and realized that the tax cut was an *illusion*; they would owe more at tax time.

24.09. Which sentence uses the italicized word correctly?

b) The judge announced that Carolyn had been selected as an *alternate* juror.

24.10. Which sentence is written correctly?

c) The senator made an *allusion* to the tax benefits included in the proposed legislation.

24.11. Which sentence is written correctly?

b) The bank robber's *elusion* of detectives enabled him to rob yet another bank in Iowa.

24.12. Which passage uses both italicized words correctly?

a) The doctor made several *allusions* to a diet plan and warned the obese patient that he should have no *illusions* about over-the-counter medications being of much benefit.

24.13. Which sentence uses the italicized word correctly?

b) No *alternative* energy source is as cheap as natural gas.

24.14. Which sentence uses the italicized word correctly?

a) The student dropped out of college, announcing that she wanted to pursue an *alternative* lifestyle.

24.15. *Anticipate* and *expect* have the same meaning and can be used interchangeably.

b) False

24.16. Which sentence is written correctly?

b) It was rumored that Megan was homesick and wanted to be back in New York *among* friends.

24.17. Which sentence is written correctly?

a) I gave Jessica and Pierre some cake and told them to share it *between* them.

24.18. Which secluded campsite is described correctly?

a) The secluded campsite is hidden *among* the pine trees.

24.19. Which statement is written correctly?

b) I don't taste a difference *between* the red apples and the yellow ones.

24.20. Which sentence uses the italicized word correctly?

a) The Google Maps app directed me to take an *alternate* route to reach my destination.

24.21. The difference between *anybody* and *anyone* is subtle but distinct. The former means "any human" and can encompass a group of people; the latter means "any one person."

a) True

24.22. Which construction is grammatically preferable?

b) You must *get in touch* with your math professor to discuss your exam grade.

24.23. The expression *as yet* should only be used at the beginning of a sentence. For instance: *As yet (or so far), the wildflowers have not bloomed.*

a) True

24.24. Which sentence is written correctly?

b) Senator McAllen is widely regarded *as* the most conservative member on the committee.

24.25. The expression *and/or* is a lazy shortcut that often creates ambiguity and should be avoided in writing.

a) True

24.26. Which construction is grammatically correct?

b) The local election results have not been announced *yet*.

24.27. Which sentence is written correctly?

b) Magdalena *could not care less* about her parents' opinion.

24.28. The problem with the phrase *I could care less* is that it is missing the word *not* and thus implies that you do care, and thus it is possible for you to care less.

a) True

24.29. The word *comprise* means "to contain" or "to be made up of." For example, "The house comprises five rooms" means it contains five rooms.

a) True

24.30. The expression *currently* is usually redundant and should be written out of every sentence.

a) True

24.31. Which one of the following sentences avoids redundancy?

c) The company is accepting applications for the position of senior engineer.

24.32. Which sentence uses *disinterested* correctly?

c) The court-appointed mediator should be a *disinterested* party in the dispute.

24.33. If you are *disinterested*, it means you are _____.

d) impartial

24.34. The expression *each and every one* should be avoided in most forms of writing.

a) True

24.35. The word *infer* means hinting at something, and *imply* means making an educated guess.

b) False

24.36. Which sentence contains a grammar error that writers should avoid?

a) Each and every one of those men worked hard for their wages.

24.37. Which sentence conveys Jose's enthusiasm using proper grammar?

c) Jose was enthusiastic about receiving his law degree.

24.38. Which sentence is written correctly?

a) The newspaper should publish its expose of corruption in our city, *regardless* of the fallout that might occur.

24.39. Which sentence offers the most clarity on the event being described.

b) The convict escaped from the courthouse and fled into the woods.

24.40. Which form uses *further* correctly?

a) The astronomer delved *further* into the mysterious signal from deep space.

24.41. Which sentence uses the word *farther* correctly?

b) The two men jogged for one hour, but the older man ran *farther* than the younger man.

24.42. In most instances, the term *facility* should be replaced with a more descriptive noun; for example, write "court" or "school-house" instead.

a) True

24.43. Which construction uses *gratuitous* incorrectly?

d) None of these sentences are written incorrectly.

24.44. Which sentence uses the italicized word correctly?

a) The stock broker *implied* that his client's entire investment might be at risk.

24.45. Which sentence uses the italicized word correctly?

c) Neither sentence is written correctly.

24.46. Which sentence uses the italicized word correctly?

a) Am I right to *infer* that you think I am a lousy writer?

24.47. You should use the expression *inside of* only in the adverbial sense of "in less than," as, "I will be home inside of an hour." Otherwise, you should omit "of" and simply write "inside."

a) True

24.48. Which sentence is written correctly?

c) Most important, your lottery prize will be paid in cash.

24.49. The word *nauseated* means "causing nausea," and *nauseous* means "feeling sick."

b) False

24.50. Which sentence reflects the best grammatical style?

b) *Inside* the box, the clerk placed five cans of cleanser.

24.51. The word *insightful* is often used as an exaggeration for "perceptive" and should only be used to denote a high degree of perception that qualifies as genuine insight.

a) True

24.52. Which passage is written incorrectly?

b) *In regards to* your question, I'll do some research and get back to you with an answer.

24.53. Adding the *-ir* prefix to *regardless* forms a nonsensical expression, *irregardless*, which should never be used in writing.

a) True

24.54. Writers often confuse *lay* and *lie*, but it is easy to remember the difference in present tense: *lay* requires an object, such as you lay a book on the desk, and lie doesn't (so you lie on the grass and watch the clouds).

a) True

24.55. Which construction uses the present tense of *lie* correctly?

c) I lie down on the floor to stretch my back.

24.56. Which construction uses the past tense of *lie* correctly?

a) Yesterday, I lay there remembering our trip to Hawaii.

24.57. Which construction uses the past participle of *lie* correctly?

b) But I forgot that I had lain there the day before enjoying the same fond memory.

24.58. Which construction uses the present tense of *lay* correctly?

a) As I walk by, I lay the book on the desk.

24.59. Which sentence uses the past tense of *lay* correctly?

c) As I walked by, I laid the book on the desk.

24.60. Which construction uses the past participle of *lay* correctly?

a) I had laid the book on the desk.

24.61. Some writers confuse *leave*, which means to depart from a place, and *let*, which means to directly or inadvertently allow something to happen.

a) True

24.62. Which form is written incorrectly?

c) I thought about it, and I'm willing to *leave* it go.

24.63. As an adjective, *meaningful* is vague and threadbare. You should replace it with another more relevant or specific adjective in your writing.

a) True

24.64. Which construction is grammatically unsound?

c) Laura changed Bob's life in meaningful ways.

24.65. Which sentence is written correctly?

c) *The fact is* clear to all who read Arthur's biography.

24.66. *Nauseousness* is a medical condition that arises from a feeling of being nauseous.

b) False

24.67. *Nor* and *or* are often confused and used incorrectly in writing. Which sentence is written correctly?

d) None of the answers are written correctly.

24.68. *Ongoing* is often redundant and adds nothing to a sentence; occasionally, however, its use is appropriate. Choose the sentence in which *ongoing* is used correctly.

c) The fundraising campaign for the domestic violence shelter is *ongoing*.

24.69. *Personally* is often a threadbare adverb that adds nothing to a sentence; or it is used incorrectly as a substitute for "personal." Which sentence uses *personally* correctly?

e) None of the sentences are correct.

24.70. If you are *nauseated*, you are about to throw up. If you are *nauseous*, you are offensive and about to make someone else to throw up.

a) True

24.71. *Presently* can mean "at the present time" or "soon; in a short time." E. B. White advises that substituting the word for *currently* may lead to confusion, and *presently* should be limited to the latter meaning. If you follow that advice, which sentence uses *presently* correctly?

b) The train from Chicago will be arriving *presently*.

24.72. Which sentence is written correctly?

c) The cruise ship sank in the harbor as it embarked on its maiden voyage, which was a *regrettable* start.

24.73. Which sentence uses *that* or *which* incorrectly?

a) You must continually seek knowledge in a world *which* is constantly changing.

24.74. Which construction uses *that* or *which* incorrectly?

c) Pies *which* contain fruit fillings are my favorite dessert.

24.75. Which sentence is written correctly?

b) *The truth is* stranger than fiction.

24.76. *The foreseeable future* is a hackneyed and ambiguous expression that should be avoided in formal writing.

a) True

24.77. Which form is written incorrectly?

c) The limo driver took a *torturous* route through the city.

24.78. *Torturous* means "full of twists and turns," and *tortuous* means "involving or causing torture."

b) False

24.79. Which sentence uses *thrust* in a way that would make any grammar purist groan?

b) Mr. Miller's campaign for a seat in the state senate has tremendous *thrust*.

24.80. Which sentence is written correctly?

c) The police nabbed the bank robber after a *tortuous* chase through the underground labyrinth of sewer canals.

24.81. Which phrase is grammatically correct?

e) None of the sentences are written correctly—if something is unique, it's one of a kind, with no comparison.

24.82. It is acceptable to write either *try and* or *try to* ("try and start the car," "try to start the car"); but the latter is more precise and should be used in formal writing.

a) True

24.83. Which sentence is written correctly?

a) You must *try to repair* the broken window in the kitchen before the storm arrives on Friday.

24.84. The word *unique* has a superlative form, so it is proper to write that something is unique, very unique, more unique, or the most unique.

b) False

24.85. The words *use* and *utilize* mean the same and may be used interchangeably in your writing.

b) False

24.86. To *utilize* something means to employ it for a certain purpose; to *use* something means to employ it in a creative, unexpected, or exemplary way.

b) False

24.87. Which sentence is written correctly?

a) Do you have a pencil I can *use*?

24.88. Which sentence is written correctly?

a) I can *utilize* my hairbrush to remove snow from the windshield.

24.89. Which construction is grammatically preferable?

b) Although it was the busiest time of the year for retail, Mr. Jones promised his family that he would *try to take off* the weekend.

23.90. Which sentence is written correctly?

b) What kind of shovel can I *use* to remove the snow?

24.91. Which sentence uses the italicized word correctly?

b) Maryanne *used* the flashlight to illuminate the garage.

24.92. Some writers tack the suffix *-wise* onto a plethora of nouns, but most such constructions are ill-advised. One of the few exceptions to this rule is in the word *clockwise*.

a) True

Quiz #25 Answers

25.01. The taxi driver _____ veered off the winding country road and into the ditch.

b) accidentally

25.02. The historic role of the United States Senate is to _____ and consent.

a) advise

25.03. Mr. Lopez, the guidance counselor at our college, always gives good _____.

c) advice

25.04. The jet suddenly made a U-turn and changed _____.

b) course

25.05. The gloomy weather in Seattle may tend to _____ your mood.

a) affect

25.06. The fraudster was able to _____ his victims.

b) deceive

25.07. _____ must evacuate the building at once!

a) Everyone

25.08. The detective surmised that _____ of those men might be the thief.

b) any one

25.09. _____ who ventures into that remote wilderness risks being killed by hostile natives or wild beasts.

a) Anyone

25.10. When I go to the grocery store, it is hard to _____ food costs so much.

c) believe

25.11. The wealthy industrialist's substantial donations _____ a worthy cause.

b) benefit

25.12. The protesters accomplished their goal at the rally, which was to _____ the status quo.

a) challenge

25.13. That grade of sandpaper is very _____.

c) coarse

25.14. That supervisor is not well liked because he will often _____ his workers.

c) criticize

25.15. It might be hard to fathom, but there is a _____ moral to this story.

a) definite

25.16. The detective asked, "Can you _____ the man who robbed the bank?"

a) describe

25.17. Some people fear the unknown and _____ what they do not understand.

b) despise

25.18. According to the weather forecast, a major snowstorm is expected to _____ over the Rockies tonight.

b) develop

25.19. You will surely _____ yourself if you wear that dress out in public.

b) embarrass

25.20. The young girl tried very hard not to _____ her parents.

a) disappoint

25.21. An hour after dawn, the dense fog began to _____.

c) dissipate

25.22. That small bolt serves a ____ purpose.

a) dual

25.23. A feeling of _____ came over the climber when he reached the mountain top.

b) ecstasy

25.24. The acclaimed physicist affirmed his belief in the _____ of extraterrestrial life.

c) existence

25.25. The tranquilizer had no _____ on the raging bull.

a) effect

25.26. It might surprise you, but I have read _____ of Stephen King's books.

b) every one

25.27. Tragically, _____ of the turtles that washed up on the shore was frozen.

b) every one

25.28. That man has the power to _____ every woman he meets.

c) fascinate

25.29. The four-story office building was destroyed by a _____ explosion.

b) fiery

25.30. That police detective was _____ a Navy seal.

a) formerly

25.31. To be honest, Ted's joke was not _____ and no one laughed.

a) humorous

25.32. The politician's _____ was on full display when he contradicted what he had said last week and denied his prior claim.

c) hypocrisy

25.33. When a ghostly hand hurled a glass vase across the room and it shattered against the fireplace mantle, the terrified girl _____ ran outdoors.

b) immediately

25.34. That man is not a police officer—he's an _____!

b) impostor

25.35. The bizarre _____ made Tyrone and his friends fear for their lives.

a) incident

25.36. That scientific theory was discussed at the seminar, but only _____.

c) incidentally

25.37. Vitamins C and D are both essential, but the _____ is a hormone, not a vitamin.

a) latter

25.38. If you _____ your keys, you will be locked out of your house and will need to call a locksmith.

b) lose

25.39. William and Lucy reaffirmed their _____ vows at a romantic getaway in Hawaii.

b) marriage

25.40. The children always seem to get into _____ when they are left alone for more than a few minutes.

a) mischief

25.41. Dr. Fung diagnosed the patient with indigestion and a heart _____.

b) murmur

25.42. Like it or not, it's a fact that money is a _____ evil in today's world.

a) necessary

25.43. The tragic accident on the bridge _____ early last month.

b) occurred

25.44. If you want _____ to come knocking, you must be ready and willing to answer the door.

b) opportunity

25.45. Did Einstein believe that humans exist here on earth and at the same time coexist in a _____ universe?

a) parallel

25.46. Neil Simon was a prolific _____.

b) playwright

25.47. In the weeks _____ the election, pollsters made wildly differing predictions about the outcome.

c) preceding

25.48. The man's vile remarks revealed the depth of his _____ and hatred of his neighbors.

c) prejudice

25.49. Ms. Chang, the high school _____, expelled both students for vaping in the bathroom.

a) principal

25.50. Though controversial, that scientific _____ is based on solid evidence.

b) principle

25.51. In America, voting is a right, and driving a car is a _____.

a) privilege

25.52. The woman seemed quite happy as she read her child's favorite nursery _____.

c) rhyme

25.53. Vanessa might _____ a degree in law.

b) pursue

25.54. Making the same point three times in an essay is unnecessary _____.

c) repetition

25.55. Uncle Bill had no sense of _____ whatsoever and made a fool of himself on the dance floor.

b) rhythm

25.56. That is a ____ excuse for missing work!

b) ridiculous

25.57. Many church leaders condemned the book as _____.

c) sacrilegious

25.58. The barbarian invaders attempted to _____ the palace but were repelled by the king's brave fighters.

b) seize

25.59. The two strangers met, exchanged a few words, and then went their _____ ways.

a) separate

25.60. As the weather turned cold, the _____ collected his flock and brought them down from the hills.

b) shepherd

25.61. The Roman army laid _____ to the castle, and then they waited patiently for everyone inside to starve.

a) siege

25.62. Those two women look _____ in a number of ways, but it is obvious they are not related.

c) similar

25.63. A form of metaphor, a _____ is a figure of speech that compares one thing to another.

b) simile

25.64. _____ has passed since we met for coffee at the local cafe.

a) Some time

25.65. I will spend _____ in Dublin when I visit Ireland.

a) some time

25.66. We will go on a vacation _____ soon.

b) sometime

25.67. You can plainly see that the computer is gone, so _____ must have taken it.

a) someone

25.68. Roberto was just _____ smart for his own good.

c) too

25.69. He bought _____ coffees, but drank only one.

a) two

25.70. What happened to Megan was a _____, but she made the best of it.

b) tragedy

25.71. Anya is _____ guilty of shoplifting because she was caught with two bottles of perfume in her purse.

b) undoubtedly

25.72. The protagonist of a story is the hero; the antagonist is the _____.

c) villain

Quiz #26 Answers

26.01. You've no doubt heard the old adage that _____ makes the heart grow fonder.

c) absence

26.02. Professor Kirk gave the essay a C grade because the student's work was _____ but not exemplary.

b) acceptable

26.03. The chair was not sturdy enough to _____ the large man's weight, and it collapsed when he sat on it.

b) accommodate

26.04. The doctor wanted to _____ an understanding of the patient's symptoms before he prescribed medication.

b) acquire

26.05. If you want to elevate yourself from an _____ to a pro writer, you must first learn the fundamental rules of grammar.

a) amateur

26.06. The man began shouting and throwing food at frightened diners in the restaurant for no _____ reason.

b) apparent

26.07. Polar bears are struggling to survive, and many are dying of starvation, as temperatures rise in the _____ wilderness.

c) arctic

26.08. It was a pointless _____ because the neighbors shouted threats and obscenities at one another, and nothing was settled.

b) argument

26.09. One who does not believe in a supreme deity is referred to as an _____.

b) atheist

26.10. Every life has a _____ and an end. If we are lucky, many years will transpire between the two, and at least some of those years will be happy ones.

c) beginning

26.11. Samsung and Intel are the world's largest chipmakers, and they are the _____ for the PC market.

c) bellwether

26.12. Timothy burst into tears when he noticed that his _____ had been stolen, even though he had locked the chain.

b) bicycle

26.13. Former president George H. W. Bush intensely disliked _____ and once said that he never, ever, wanted to see another sprig of it on his plate

b) broccoli

26.14. Be sure to make a note of your appointment on the _____, or you might forget it.

a) calendar

26.15. The weather _____ predicted the approaching storm would bring sub-zero temperatures to the region.

a) bureau

26.16. Fernando sat at his desk, gazing up at the _____ and daydreaming rather than focusing on his math test, which was timed, and which he was almost certain to fail.

c) ceiling

26.17. Laura took flowers to the _____ and placed them on her father's grave to honor his memory.

b) cemetery

26.18. Some states in the U.S. are suffering from extreme drought, but weather is _____, and the winter months could make the situation better or worse.

c) changeable

26.19. Every one of the athletes had a strong sense of _____ and mutual respect for her teammates.

b) camaraderie

26.20. Every employer wants to hire _____ employees who are honest, dependable, and work hard.

c) conscientious

26.21. The doctor informed us of our uncle's _____, and we all were stunned by the news.

b) decease

26.22. The saying, "Let your _____ be your guide is often thought to derive from the Bible; in fact, it is from Disney's story of *Pinocchio*.

b) conscience

26.23. The clinical trial reported that patients were grouped into more than one _____, depending on their symptoms and the degree of severity.

c) category

26.24. What is lacking in our leaders today is a _____ of opinion on how to approach immigration reform.

b) consensus

26.25. The investigative journalist sparked an uproar when he published a story in his newspaper _____, alleging that the pharmaceutical company knew its drug was unsafe and conspired to hide the truth.

a) column

26.26. Lisa's favorite drink is the strawberry _____, but she can never stop at just one.

a) daiquiri

26.27. Some believe that parents who fail to _____ their children do more harm than good; others disagree.

b) discipline

26.28. Driving up the mountain, we found that our car guzzled gasoline; but during our _____ down the other side, we coasted most of the way.

b) descent

26.29. Renters throughout California are in _____ need of affordable housing.

c) desperate

26.30. A bolt of lightning struck the tree with _____ consequences—less than thirty minutes later, a massive forest fire raged out of control.

c) disastrous

26.31. The CEO _____ perjury because he lied on the witness stand under oath, and the prosecutor had evidence to prove it.

a) committed

26.32. When the patrol car passed by and the policeman saw the man stumbling down the street, he was arrested for public _____.

a) drunkenness

26.33. Learning a _____ language can be a daunting task, though some languages are easier to learn than others.

b) foreign

26.34. The farmer moved his tractor and other _____ into the barn the day before the first winter snow fell.

b) equipment

26.35. If you want to be healthy and live to a ripe old age, it is imperative that you _____ for at least a half hour every day.

a) exercise

26.36. The blue sky, the sound of the waves, the sea breeze, and the vast ocean melting into the horizon will _____ you the first time, and perhaps every time, you see it.

a) exhilarate

26.37. It is often said that _____ is the best teacher; but learning by trial and error is not the easiest way.

c) experience

26.38. Abraham Lincoln and George Washington both were born in the month of _____.

c) February

26.39. LED light bulbs cost more to buy than fluorescent bulbs, but they are cheaper to operate and do not contain mercury, which can pose serious health hazards.

b) fluorescent

26.40. While exercising, your hands may become sweaty and you could lose your grip on the _____, dropping it on your foot.

b) dumbbell

26.41. It is difficult to _____ a person's intentions from one conversation; but as the saying goes, actions speak louder than words.

c) gauge

26.42. If you want to be at peace with life, a conscience and a well-defined moral compass are _____.

c) indispensable

26.43. Many manufacturers offer a written _____ that their products will perform as intended for a certain amount of time.

c) guarantee

26.44. "The true sign of _____ is not knowledge but imagination." —Albert Einstein

a) intelligence

26.45. Abby was _____ for the opportunity to move away from the Midwest cornfields and to start a new life in California.

b) grateful

26.46. The #MeToo movement put employers on notice that they can no longer _____ workers with impunity, and supervisors who behave inappropriately in the workplace may be sued or even prosecuted.

a) harass

26.47. "Every human has four endowments—self-awareness, conscience, _____ will, and creative imagination. These give us the ultimate human freedom...The power to choose, to respond, to change." —Stephen Covey

b) independent

26.48. Nietzsche observed: "All sciences are now under the obligation to prepare the ground for the future task of the philosopher, which is to solve the problem of value, to determine the true _____ of values."

a) hierarchy

26.49. To adjust the _____ of the chair, simply lift up on the lever under the seat.

b) height

26.50. You must have a driver's _____ to legally operate a vehicle on public streets.

c) license

26.51. The flood waters pose no _____ danger to any of the homes in the area.

c) immediate

26.52. The Pentagon has ordered enough vaccine to _____ soldiers who might be exposed to smallpox or anthrax in a war zone.

b) inoculate

26.53. A recent survey on dating found that over 75% of the respondents admitted that their dating partners had done something that made them _____.

b) jealous

26.54. "Nothing in all the world is more dangerous than sincere _____ and conscientious stupidity." —Martin Luther King Jr.

c) ignorance

26.55. Rings, necklaces, and bracelets are common forms of _____.

c) jewelry

26.56. "The goal of education is not to increase the amount of _____ but to create the possibilities for a child to invent and discover, to create men who are capable of doing new things."—Jean Piaget

a) knowledge

26.57. For some, writing is a _____ pastime, while for others, it is a compulsion.

b) leisure

26.58. David and Karen became lovers and best friends, and the _____ lasted for many years.

a) liaison

26.59. "The world is full of a lot of fear and a lot of negativity, and a lot of _____. I just think people need to start shifting into joy and happiness. As corny as it sounds, we need to make a shift." —Ellen DeGeneres

b) judgment

26.60. The dealer informed Isabella that she should bring her car to the shop for an oil change and _____ every 5,000 miles.

c) maintenance

26.61. The carpenter's toolbox contained hammers, screwdrivers, a wrench, and _____ odds and ends

b) miscellaneous

26.62. Geometry, calculus and trigonometry are advanced forms of _____.

b) mathematics

26.63. Swords, daggers, and battle axes were common weapons in _____ times.

a) medieval

26.64. The taxi driver was able to deftly _____ his cab through rush hour traffic.

b) maneuver

26.65. The band's performance was _____ at best, and most of the crowd left after the first couple of songs.

a) mediocre

26.66. A greeting card or a snapshot can make the perfect _____ for a scrapbook.

b) memento

26.67. A period of 100 years is a century, and a period of 1,000 years is a _____.

c) millennium

26.68. Household dust is typically made up of _____ various substances, including pollen, blowing soil, pet dander, dust mites and their excrement, decomposing insects, human hair, and skin flakes.

c) minuscule

26.69. My sister in Texas has an adorable _____ poodle named Gracie.

b) miniature

26.70. Shelby flashed her boyfriend a _____ smile, knowing he would he amused by the practical joke she was about to play.

a) mischievous

26.71. As the rain intensified, accompanied by thunder and lightning, a _____ shadow hovered in the dark alcove outside the industrialist's mansion.

b) mysterious

26.72. Mr. Zhao was always cordial to his _____, but he instinctively disliked the man and did not trust him.

b) neighbor

26.73. The scratch in the new table top is quite _____, and the table should be returned for a replacement.

c) noticeable

26.74. Melinda chose this _____ to announce that she and her fiancé had eloped.

b) occasion

26.75. The hope for world _____ has become elusive in today's chaotic world.

b) piece

26.76. Fish falling from the sky was a bizarre and unexpected _____ that sent terrified villagers fleeing in all directions.

c) occurrence

26.77. The priest renounced his ministry, declared himself a Buddhist, and embarked upon an _____ of discovery in Tibet.

c) odyssey

26.78. It takes planning and _____ to succeed. A bit of luck is helpful too.

b) perseverance

26.79. When the union voted to strike, the CEO made some _____ changes and fired all of his employees the next day.

a) personnel

26.80. According to the Doomsday Clock, maintained by the world's top atomic scientists, global events in 2018 have brought us closer than ever to the threat of _____ war.

a) nuclear

26.81. The birds that you are seeing out in the field are crows, sparrows, blue jays, and one large _____.

b) pigeon

26.82. It might surprise you to know that the _____ and several other edible fruits are plant species in the rose family.

b) raspberry

26.83. Which entrée on the menu do you _____?

b) recommend

26.84. "Even though it is more blessed to give than to _____, sometimes you need to be the object of someone else's compassion." —J. Earp

c) receive

26.85. The patient described her symptoms, and the doctor _____ her to a specialist.

a) referred

26.86. Dining out at a _____ is fun but more expensive than cooking meals at home.

c) restaurant

26.87. Despite the candidate's busy _____, she made time to visit a hospital, a school for disadvantaged children, and a nursing home.

b) schedule

26.88. You cannot cut down that tree with _____, no matter how determined you might be.

b) scissors

26.89. The drill _____ barked commands and made the new recruits march until they were about to collapse from exhaustion.

c) sergeant

26.90. Her son did a _____ job of washing the dinner dishes, even though he complained the whole time that his sister should have been doing the chore.

a) thorough

26.91. The woman had toiled for years to lift herself out of poverty, and now, as she stood of the _____ of success, she knew that she would never forget her humble roots.

b) threshold

26.92. The fighter jet passed _____ the clouds as it descended toward the runway.

c) through

26.93. The _____ forecast for tomorrow predicts rain, hail and freezing temperatures.

b) weather

26.94. Angry that the fast food restaurant had run out of ketchup, the customer shouted obscenities and _____ his hamburger against the wall before storming out.

a) threw

26.95. That commercial was the _____ in less than fifteen minutes—it's no wonder so many people are turning off their TVs!

c) twelfth

26.96. "Help! Why is _____ spelled like that?"—Blake Shelton

b) Wednesday

26.97. It has been said that we do not live our lives in a _____. Every thought we have, every action we take, has an effect on others around us.

c) vacuum

26.98. We will go for a drive to the mountains tomorrow, _____ it rains or not.

b) whether

26.99. "So you're a little _____? Work it! A little different? Own it! Better to be a nerd than one of the herd!"—Mandy Hale

c) weird

26.100. "The secret of freedom lies in educating people, whereas the secret of _____ is in keeping them ignorant." — Maximilien Robespierre

b) tyranny

Quiz #27 Answers

27.01. No matter how badly you want to write, no matter how deep your feelings, and no matter how exciting the ideas you want to share with others, if you don't know the basic rules of how to correctly form sentences and the relation of words to one another, your writing will lack coherency.

a) True

27.02. The author of *The Elements of Style* was _____.

d) an English professor at Cornell University

27.03. When Prof. Strunk sold the publication rights for his grammar handbook to a textbook publisher, he expected it would be a best seller and, eventually, a classic.

b) False

27.04. Strunk's grammar book stresses the importance of writing grammatically correct prose and thus offers a blueprint students and writers can follow to express their ideas in a crisp, concise, and effective manner.

a) True

27.05. The clearer your writing, the more likely it is that readers will fail to grasp the points you are trying to make.

b) False

27.06. To write correctly and effectively, a working grasp of the fundamentals of English grammar is not as important as possessing a rich vocabulary and a creative disposition.

b) False

27.07. Learning how to write correctly should be an easy challenge considering that the average person's vocabulary consists of a mere _____.

a) 2,000 words

27.08. Many of the grammar rules in Strunk's book are as valid today as they were a century ago; but, the world has changed, and the English language has changed with it, making some of those rules obsolete.

a) True

27.09. Shakespeare's classic works contain about 15,000 different words, but more than _____ of those words are obsolete today.

c) 10,000

27.10. *The Elements of Style* was written by:

c) William Strunk Jr.

27.11. The fundamental rules of grammar should be diligently followed so that you can express your thoughts and ideas in a clear and effective manner.

a) True

27.12. It has been said that the best way to learn to write is to write nothing until you have mastered the fundamentals of English grammar.

b) False

27.13. To understand the proper placement of words in sentences, it is important to know that all words in the English language are grouped into _____ categories, called "the parts of speech."

b) nine

27.14. A _____ refers to the name of any person, place, or thing, which includes tangible objects and abstract concepts.

a) noun

27.15. _____ nouns are formal names, as the names of people (John, Mary, Bob); places (London, Paris, Seattle); and countries (Canada, England, Mexico).

b) Proper

27.16. English has four articles: *a* (or *an*), *the*, *this,* and *that*.

b) False

27.17. _____ denotes clear expression of thoughts conveyed in unequivocal language, so there is no misunderstanding of the idea that the writer wishes to express.

a) Perspicuity

27.18. The _____ is the most important of the nine parts of speech, as all the rest are more or less dependent upon it.

d) noun

27.19. An _____ is a word placed before a noun to show whether the noun is used in a particular or general sense.

b) article

27.20. Nouns fall into two categories: proper and _____.

c) common

27.21. Nouns, adjectives, verbs, and adverbs become interjections when they are uttered as one-word exclamations.

a) True

27.22. Adverbs are typically used to express in one word what would otherwise require two or more words.

a) True

27.23. The article "a" is called the indefinite article because it does not refer to a particular person or thing but indicates the noun in its most general sense; for instance, *a man* can mean any man on the planet.

a) True

27.24. Consider these short phrases: a *black* dog, a *pretty* woman, a *cold* wind. The italicized words are _____.

c) adjectives

27.25. Consider this sentence: "John gave *his* pen to James, and then *he* lent it to Jane to write *her* copy with *it*." The italicized words in this sentence are:

b) pronouns

27.26. Prepositions are usually placed before words whose connection or relation with other words they point out.

a) True

27.27. The singular _____ are: *I, me, my, mine; you, your, yours; he, him, his; she, her, hers;* and *it, its.*

d) pronouns

27.28. A _____ is a word that signifies action or the doing of something; or it may be a word that affirms, commands, or asks a question.

b) verb

27.29. _____ refers to the use of proper English. It means writing without the use of slang and expletives (except when writing fiction and then used sparingly), obsolete terms, foreign idioms, ambiguous expressions, and grammatically incorrect language.

d) Purity

27.30. The words *we, us, our, ours; you, your, yours;* and *they, them, their, theirs* are plural _____.

c) pronouns

27.31. A/an _____ is a word used in place of a noun so that you don't have to repeat the same noun too often and fall into tedious repetition.

c) pronoun

27.32. Consider this sentence: "John *struck* the table with his fist." What is the italicized word?

a) a verb

27.33. An _____ is a word that modifies a verb, an adjective, or another adverb.

c) adverb

27.34. Consider this sentence: "He writes *well.*" The italicized word is _____.

d) an adverb

27.35. You should never use active voice when you can use the passive.

b) False

27.36. Pronouns fall into two categories:

c) singular and plural

27.37. If it is possible to cut a word out, you should always cut it out.

a) True

27.38. Consider this sentence: "He is *remarkably* diligent." The italicized word is:

a) an adverb

27.39. *Fire! Nonsense! Strange! No!* These words are:

c) interjections

27.40. An _____ is a word that qualifies a noun, meaning it shows or points out some distinguishing mark or feature of the noun.

c) adjective

27.41. Consider this sentence: "She is *very* beautiful." The italicized word is _____.

b) an adverb

27.42. The three essentials of effective writing in the English language are: purity, perspicuity, and precision.

a) True

27.43. A _____ connects words, clauses, and sentences together and shows the relation between them, as:

b) preposition

27.44. Consider this sentence: "My hand is *on* the table." The italicized word is _____.

a) a preposition

27.45. A/an _____ is a word that joins words, phrases, clauses, and sentences together.

d) conjunction

27.46. Consider this sentence: "John *and* James are close friends." The italicized word is _____.

c) a conjunction

27.47. Consider this sentence: "My father *and* mother arrived at the recital, *but* I did not see them." The italicized words are _____.

a) conjunctions

27.48. Consider this sentence: "I prefer apples *or* strawberries, *and* Tyrone prefers oranges." The italicized words are _____.

c) conjunctions

27.49. A/an _____ is a word that expresses surprise, shock, or some other sudden emotion.

c) interjection

27.50. This celebrated author offered poignant advice on grammar and style to writers in his discourse on *Politics and the English Language*.

d) George Orwell

27.51. Consider this sentence: *"Ah!* There he comes." The italicized word is _____.

a) an interjection

27.52. _____ requires concise and exact expression, free from redundancy–a style that is clear and simple enough so that the reader can immediately comprehend the meaning of the writer's words.

a) Precision

27.53. Consider this sentence: *"Alas!* What shall I do? *Ah!* There he comes!" The italicized words are _____.

d) interjections

27.54. The most common _____ are: *and, also; either, or; neither, nor; though, yet; but, however; for, that; because, since; therefore, wherefore, then,* and *if.*

c) conjunctions

27.55. _____ requires a style that is clear and concise, which means ambiguous words, words of double meaning, and words that might be construed in a sense different from that intended should be avoided.

b) Perspicuity

27.56. You should never use a foreign phrase, a scientific word, or jargon if you can think of an everyday English equivalent to use instead.

a) True

-The End-

Elements of Style 2017

Edited by Richard De A'Morelli

(Nonfiction Reference/Writing)

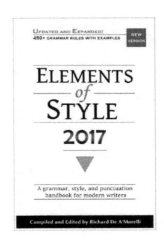

Elements of Style 2017 presents a collection of grammar, style, and punctuation rules to help you to write well, self-edit efficiently, and produce a grammar-perfect final draft. It is a major update to William Strunk's classic 1921 grammar book. Much has changed in the world since then—some of the rules in Strunk's book are obsolete, and many new grammar and style rules have come into play that writers must know.

Bestselling author/editor Richard De A'Morelli shares his 30+ years of experience as a senior editor and explains what you need to know about grammar and style in a clear and simple way. Written in plain English, with easy-to-follow examples, this book takes the headache out of great writing. Read any chapter, follow the practical advice, and you will see an overnight improvement in your writing. Read a chapter a day, and in just a few weeks, you will be amazed by the polished quality of your final draft.

If you write anything at all for work, school, or your own enjoyment, you should have a copy of this writer's handbook on your desk. Learn how to improve your grammar and polish your writing to perfection with *Elements of Style 2017*.

Buy online or visit: https://books.spectrum.org/#elements

ISBN Numbers	**Editions**
978-1-988236-26-1	Kindle E-book
978-1-988236-28-5	Paperback

Printed in the USA
CPSIA information can be obtained
at www.ICGtesting.com
LVHW011916031123
762894LV00008B/655